SIMON ROSENBLUM

Misguided Missiles

Canada, the Cruise and Star Wars

James Lorimer & Company, Publishers
Toronto 1985

Copyright © 1985 by James Lorimer & Company, Publishers.

All rights reserved. No part of this book may be reproduced or transmitted in any form or by any means, electronic or mechanical, including photocopying, or by any information storage or retrieval system, without permission in writing from the publisher.

Cover design: Brant Cowie
Cover illustration: *The Egg* by Kelly Freas. Reproduced with kind permission of the artist.

Canadian Cataloguing in Publication Data

Rosenblum, Simon.
  Misguided missiles

(Canadian issues series)

ISBN 0-88862-699-1 (bound) — ISBN 0-88862-698-3 (pbk.)

1. Cruise missiles. 2. Canada — Military policy. 3. United States — Military policy. 4. Ballistic missile defences — United States. I. Title. II. Series: Canadian issues series (Toronto, Ont.).

UG1312.C7R67 1985   358'. 17'0971   C84-098208-9

James Lorimer & Company, Publishers
Egerton Ryerson Memorial Building
35 Britain Street
Toronto, Ontario M5A 1R7

Printed and bound in Canada
5 4 3 2 1   85 86 87 88 89

155-210

Misguided
Missiles

WITHDRAWN

The Canadian Issues Series

James Lorimer & Company has developed this series of original paperbacks to offer informed, up-to-date, critical introductions to key issues facing Canadians. Books are written specifically for the series by authors commissioned by the publisher on the basis of their expertise in a subject area and their ability to write for a general audience.

The 4" x 7" paperback format and cover design for the series offer attractive books at the lowest possible price. Special library hard-bound editions are also available. New titles are added to the series every spring and fall: watch for them in your local bookstore.

Already in print:
  Canada's Colonies BY KENNETH COATES
  Police BY JOHN SEWELL
  Ethics and Economics BY GREGORY BAUM and
    DUNCAN CAMERON
  The West BY J. F. CONWAY
  Oil and Gas BY JAMES LAXER
  Women and Work BY PAUL and ERIN PHILLIPS
  The New Canadian Constitution BY DAVID MILNE
  Regional Disparities BY PAUL PHILLIPS
  Out of Work BY CY GONICK
  Rising Prices BY H. LUKIN ROBINSON
  Industry in Decline BY RICHARD STARKS

Acknowledgements

It is always a pleasure to acknowledge one's indebtedness to friends and colleagues, for knowledge and understanding are best advanced by co-operation and dialogue. I owe a particular debt of gratitude to three people: to my Project Ploughshares colleague Ernie Regehr, for his insightful reflections on the arms race and his willingness to share them; to my editor Ted Mumford, who had to put up with my tardiness and who made this a much better book than it would have been without him; and to my great friend Carmen Sirianni who, while living in another country, continues to be as close as the phone on my desk.

In a world whose tenure is hardly secure, I hope this book will add a new meaning to the old academic maxim, "publish or perish."

Finally, I would like to dedicate this book to my parents, Fanny and Arthur Rosenblum, for their continuing love and support.

Introduction

It is *not* business as usual in the nuclear arms race. In 1984, the *Bulletin of Atomic Scientists* moved its "doomsday clock" forward by one minute. It is now three minutes before midnight. We are on the threshold of the most dangerous upward spiral in the history of the nuclear arms race.

The source of this increased danger is a series of technological advances in nuclear weapons and auxiliary systems — and the uses that are being planned for them. Two systems at the crest of this new wave are the Cruise missile and the American Strategic Defense Initiative — popularly known as "Star Wars." Both the Cruise and Star Wars fit into the new doctrine of "nuclear war-fighting," and draw Canada into American schemes to reassert nuclear dominance. The two provide the framework for this book's examination of how the arms race feeds on itself.

The sheer size of nuclear arsenals exclusive of these advances is of course frightening. Recent studies have demonstrated that the use of only a small proportion of the superpowers' stockpiles could produce a "nuclear winter" — the end of human life on this planet. Now that extinction is easily within our grasp, the danger is not so much how much bigger the arsenals get, but the effect of new components and strategies: they provide the spark next to the powderkeg.

The Pretext of Deterrence

Theories about the relative strengths of Soviet and American nuclear arsenals and the deterrent they supply are regularly used to rationalize new systems like the Cruise and Star Wars. The doctrine of deterrence holds that nuclear attack is deterred by the promise of massive retaliation — "mutually assured destruction," or MAD. As long as arsenals are balanced, so the theory goes, an attack is unthinkable.

The Reagan administration in the United States has gained support for its rearmament program by alleging that the American capacity for deterrence has eroded, creating a "window of vulnerability" which the Russians, now enjoying a "margin of nuclear superiority" (President Reagan's words), can exploit to their advantage.

Yet a wide range of analyses have shown that the U.S. is not actually "behind" the USSR. An accounting by the Washington-based Arms Control Association in June of 1985 found that the USSR leads the U.S. overall in "launchers" (i.e., land-based and submarine-launched intercontinental ballistic missiles, as well as bombers) by 2,495 to 1,928. But in the more significant category of warheads — the number of nuclear bombs that can hit individual targets — the U.S. leads. The USSR has somewhere between 7,868 and 9,644 warheads, depending on counting methods; the U.S. has either 10,983 or 11,183.

If vulnerability exists, it is the Soviets who should be worried, since they have fully two-thirds of their nuclear arsenal deployed on increasingly vulnerable land-based missiles. By contrast, the U.S. has only a quarter of its arsenal so deployed. Meanwhile the U.S. constantly maintains 3,000 of its 5,000-plus sea-based nuclear weapons out of port and ready for firing. The Soviets can keep only about 300 such weapons (out of a total of 2,000) in this state of readiness.

The "who's ahead" equation also ought to take into account the technological superiority that gives U.S. weapons more accuracy and hence a greater capacity to destroy military targets. The U.S. is not about to lose that edge. According to Richard DeLauer, former U.S. under-secretary of defense for research and development, the U.S. leads the USSR overall in basic technologies that have the potential to affect the military balance over the next ten to twenty years. The U.S. surpasses the USSR in thirteen of twenty specific categories of technology, and the two nations are neck and neck in five more. Military officials can't hide this light under a bushel. During Senate Foreign Relations Committee hearings in 1982, Senator Charles Percy asked Defense Secretary Caspar Weinberger which arsenal he would prefer to have. Weinberger answered, "I would not for a moment exchange anything because we have an immense edge in technology."

The alleged American weakness is one of vulnerability to a Soviet first strike. The USSR is indeed now deploying missiles with sufficient accuracy to threaten U.S. land-based missiles. But even in the most "successful" pre-emptive attack by the USSR, some U.S. land-based missiles would survive. So would substantial numbers of nuclear bombers and virtually all U.S. sea-based nuclear weapons. The American retaliatory capacity would still be of extraordinary dimensions. For example, the Centre for Defense

Information notes that even if the USSR could destroy most U.S. land-based missiles in the late 1980s, 60 per cent of the U.S. submarine force would be at sea with 3,600 weapons at the ready. This is sufficient to destroy the USSR many times over.

On the other hand, the Soviet Union is relatively vulnerable to a U.S. first strike. A 1982 analysis published in *Scientific American* estimated that after a Soviet first strike, the U.S. would have some 3,600 warheads remaining, and the USSR would still have 4,400 unused warheads. In the case of a U.S. first strike, however, the USSR would be left with only 1,200 warheads, and the U.S. stockpile would still number about 6,500. Analyses like these indicate that no additional nuclear weapons are required by the U.S. to deny the Soviet Union a first-strike capability.

Many prominent and formerly prominent defense officials are as frank as Weinberger regarding supposed Soviet strategic supremacy. Those who have asserted that the American retaliation potential is absolute include William Colby, former head of the CIA; George Kennan, former U.S. ambassador to the Soviet Union; Robert McNamara, former U.S. secretary of defense; the late Canadian Lt. Gen. E.L.M. Burns; George Ignatieff, former Canadian ambassador to the U.N.; and the members of President Reagan's own Scowcroft Commission. Retired Rear Adm. Gene LaRocque remarks that "Soviet nuclear superiority is one of the greatest myths that has ever been perpetrated on the American people."

Why does the math, and the opinions of these experts, not match White House rhetoric? For U.S. military planners, maintaining deterrence actually means maintaining decisive American superiority. All evidence suggests that the current U.S. administration believes in the nearly universal utility of military power in international diplomacy. As Reagan officials see it, the geopolitical "setbacks" of the late 1970s resulted from Washington's declining ability to wield military power with impunity. In the period following World War II, the U.S. could take this ability for granted. But after the Soviet Union gained rough military parity in the 1970s, the U.S. threat to use nuclear weapons against Soviet forces began to lose credibility in any situation other than an attack on the U.S. itself. To regain this credibility seemed to require recapturing a degree of military superiority — a technological edge over the USSR that would allow the U.S. to dominate combat at any level. Thus the impetus for the most recent military build-up came not from Soviet superiority, nor from a belief that the USSR was about to attack the U.S. or its allies, but from a desire to re-establish American pre-eminence in the arms race.

Because it is a powerful image of national security, deterrence can be invoked like motherhood and apple pie when political support for rearmament is needed. As the Centre for Defense Information laments, "The vague concept of deterrence is used to justify everything we do. It has become a meaningless slogan." Similarly, the propensity for "refinements" to this slippery concept led Theodore Draper to observe dourly that deterrence "may yet equal liberty for the number of crimes committed in its name."

When deterrence is cited to justify new weapons, it is actually a new post-deterrence doctrine that inspires them.

The New Doctrine of the Arms Race

The ability to attack rather than to defend against attack is the new cornerstone of the nuclear weapon systems of both superpowers. The governing perspective of military planners is not deterrence but nuclear warfighting. Civilian and military planners, having decided that protracted nuclear war is possible, are determined that American nuclear forces will prevail and force the USSR to seek termination of hostilities on terms favourable to the U.S. Concepts complementary to the nuclear war-fighting doctrine include the notion of "limited" nuclear war and the use of nuclear threats to project power in various locations around the world.

The Cruise missile in its various forms is one of five new nuclear missile systems that the U.S. plans to deploy in the 1980s. The other four are the Pershing II missile, the MX missile (christened the Peacemaker by President Reagan), the Trident D-5 submarine-launched missile and the "Midgetman" missile. The total Reagan plan for regaining superiority calls for 17,000 new weapons.

All of these new missiles have in common one characteristic: they are much more accurate than previous American systems and existing Soviet systems. For the first time, provided the missiles work reliably, a single warhead is virtually certain to destroy "hardened" military targets such as missile silos or command centres. This makes a first strike much more feasible. It is more feasible yet if a reliable defense system (the Star Wars notion) is in place to minimize the effect of whatever retaliation the Soviets can muster with their surviving missiles. The deployment of these new systems invites the Soviets not only to increase their own nuclear strength but to change their nuclear policy toward launch-on-warning or pre-emptive strike scenarios.

Under the new doctrine, neither side is actually planning to unleash a large-scale premeditated attack. What is much more likely is inadvertent war, war caused by miscalculation, misperceptions, or failure of communication in a time of crisis. The shortened flight time of the newer missiles reduces the opportunity for communication and control. Accordingly pressures increase to adopt stances favouring pre-emptive strikes, "launch-on-warning" and, conceivably, early use of nuclear weapons.

As well, the new sophistication has led to reliance on automated electronic early warning systems. But both computers and their operators can and do make mistakes. In one eighteen-month period, U.S. missile warning systems suffered 147 malfunctions. Soviet computers are in all likelihood even less reliable. Yet given the speed of new missiles, little time is available to confirm a computer attack warning and to decide on a response. Thus both sides will become increasingly likely to interpret warnings as the real thing and to launch all their own weapons rather than risk having them destroyed in their silos. If the warning turns out to have been a false alarm, it will be too late to turn back. A Star Wars scheme would be even more sensitive, and demanding of quick decisions and computer reliability.

The new character of missiles also increases the advantages of a first strike. In a crisis in which the superpowers are in a direct confrontation and regard a nuclear exchange as rapidly becoming inevitable, either side might consider it advantageous to strike first, for two reasons. In the first instance, each side, suspecting a surprise attack, would be tempted to fire first to prevent its missiles from being destroyed in the silos. In the second instance, a surprise first strike would be inviting as a means of eliminating as much of the other side's nuclear arsenal as possible. Such a pre-emptive strike would be viewed as limiting the other side's capacity to retaliate and offering the best chance of keeping one's own damage to "acceptable" levels.

The Cruise and Star Wars

The Cruise missile is marketed to the public as part of a necessary deterrent. In Canada, where both production of parts and flight testing for the Cruise have taken place, participation in the development of the weapon has also been upheld as part of a Canadian obligation to its major ally and to NATO. The merits of this argument will be looked at later; for now it suffices to note that while the American deterrent is already larger than necessary, quite un-defensive uses are planned for the Cruise.

While prime minister, Pierre Trudeau said that "the Cruise missile is not an aggressive weapon." But as Trudeau himself has also said, the issue is not just a weapon system's capacity for destruction but the intentions of the government that controls it. The Cruise is considered by the U.S. military to be a nuclear warfighting weapon. Because of its high accuracy and ability to evade detection, it has been assigned the task of destroying military and industrial targets in the USSR once war has started. It is also planned for use in "limited attacks," attempts to use nuclear weapons in a "controlled" manner without risking all-out nuclear war.

The Strategic Defense Initiative (SDI) is the latest development in the Pentagon's military build-up; indeed it rapidly has become central to Washington's nuclear strategies. Contrary to the claims of its promoters, "Star Wars" is neither a purely defensive technology nor an alternative to the arms race. It is an integral part of the new offensive nuclear strategy. Already it has been leaked that the Pentagon plans to integrate SDI with offensive nuclear weapons for a comprehensive nuclear war-fighting capacity. The intent is to provide nuclear flexibility, including support of a first strike or other war-fighting options, rather than nuclear defense per se.

Star Wars, like every new weapon, is an escalation of the arms race. But it is more than that. Next to the atom bomb itself, the development of a space-based anti-missile system represents the greatest single leap in nuclear war technology, because it will take war into an entirely new realm — akin to the introduction of naval or aerial warfare. The needlessness of this escalation has been condemned from many quarters. George Ball, the distinguished former U.S. under-secretary of state, has called Reagan's SDI proposal "one of the most irresponsible acts by any head of state in modern times." Over 50 Nobel Prize winners and 700 members of the National Academy of Sciences have joined a campaign to stop a program that would end, in the words of the Union of Concerned Scientists, by "dragging heaven into hell."

Both Star Wars and the Cruise greatly jeopardize prospects for nuclear arms control. Perhaps this is not surprising, since the Reagan administration has made its opposition to a nuclear freeze crystal clear, and President Reagan has never publicly supported any arms treaty agreed to thus far by the nuclear superpowers. His arms control negotiator Edward Rowny commented in 1980 that "We have put too much emphasis on the control of arms and too little on the provision of arms." And the president's arms control and disarmament director, Kenneth Adelman, pointed out in 1982 that "One reason not to rush into negotiations is that these negotiations tend to discourage money for defense programs."

The Cruise has been called "a weapon against arms control" since by nature it interferes with simple verification procedures and thus the future of arms control generally. In the eyes of the Reagan administration this is just another of the Cruise's simple virtues. Star Wars meanwhile will probably inspire the Soviets to increase their arsenal in order to saturate U.S. defenses. As with the Cruise, the Soviets are also developing an equivalent to Star Wars. In arms talks they have insisted that they won't agree to limitations until the U.S. abandons SDI — and Reagan refuses to put SDI on the table.

It is a sad fact that the U.S. could quite easily have reached an agreement with the Soviets to ban development of long-range Cruise missiles and Star Wars technology. Ironically, in the past it was the Russians who were most enthusiastic about Cruise missiles and ballistic missile defense. Washington's interest in these systems came later, and in both cases it was primarily a political impulse rather than a military purpose that sponsored their early development.

Canada's Position

At the first United Nations special session on disarmament in 1978, Prime Minister Trudeau said he was particularly concerned about the "technological impulse" behind the development of nuclear weapons. Among other things, he called for a mutual ban by the superpowers on flight testing of strategic delivery systems.

His concern was most timely. It was at this time that dramatic improvements in technology and engineering were beginning to alter the nuclear terrain. Yet it was Trudeau's own government that took a major step toward assisting in the development of the Cruise, a weapon that makes nuclear war less unthinkable (in strategic language, it lowers the "nuclear threshold").

The Canadian government has long been ambivalent about nuclear weapons. Trudeau's contradictory behaviour reaches back to the early l960s, when he had a falling out with the Liberal Party over a policy flip-flop — from rejecting to accepting nuclear weapons. While Trudeau as prime minister proclaimed at the U.N. that world security is "teetering" and "we're living in a tinder box," his defense minister, Gilles Lamontagne, argued that increased fears of nuclear war are "greatly exaggerated if not quite baseless."

Similarly, the government of Brian Mulroney has appointed disarmament advocates such as Stephen Lewis and Douglas Roche to United Nations positions but continues to view SDI as "prudent." Even when Ottawa declined formal government-to-government involvement in Star Wars in September 1985, it facilitated Canadian industrial participation and continued to run political interference for SDI in the international arena.

A twenty-six country poll by Gallup showed that Canadians were among the least optimistic on the prospects of avoiding a global war over the next ten years. But polling has also shown Canadians are divided over whether to support Canadian participation in the Cruise and Star Wars, which are assuredly raising the risk of war. This too may reflect Canadian ambivalence, or perhaps it simply reflects confusion. The federal government has not tried to inform Canadians about the implications of the Cruise and Star Wars; rather it has tried to avoid the issues or reduce them to simple matters of alliance solidarity.

Any attempt to avoid public debate on these issues is aided by the confusion over technical and strategic matters. Ken Lewis, head of an industry lobby group seeking SDI business, has gone so far as to state that the average Canadian simply isn't capable of understanding SDI. It is more likely that the mystifying effect of obscure language has been useful in excluding the public from the debate. In this book, the technical details and often jargon-ridden theories have been put into plain English to the best of the author's abilities (a glossary is included at the end of the book).

One note of caution, however, ought to be sounded concerning a curious ambivalence that characterizes much of the debate over various nuclear weapon systems. With the obvious exception of the A-bombs dropped on Japan in 1945, no nuclear strategy or weapon has been put to the test. Weapons and doctrines have been developed and become obsolete without ever being employed. Planners, strategists and, regrettably, many politicians put their trust in ever-changing abstract scenarios, each one perched atop a stack of assumptions. While there may be grave doubts about how a given weapon system will perform in actual conditions of war (this is certainly the case with the Cruise and Star Wars, as we shall see), planners assume they will work perfectly. And the planners on the other side assume this too. Taking the worst-case possibility, they mount retaliatory counter-strategies accordingly. Response and counter-response spin in ever more fantastic, and ever more dangerous, theoretical circles. Ultimately, however, it is no fantasy: even if only a fraction of the systems work in a conflict, that will be sufficient to blanket the planet with destruction.

The discussion in this book moves on the whole from the Cruise missile to the Star Wars scheme. Chapter 1 describes the history of the Cruise missile, Chapter 2 its capabilities, the technical problems it faces and the challenge it poses for arms control. Chapter 3 analyses the new doctrine of nuclear war-fighting. The European theatre, where Cruise missiles are now being deployed by NATO, is the subject of Chapter 4. Chapter 5 turns to Canada's role — in general as a participant in the arms race and specifically regarding the issues of Cruise testing and assembly. SDI is the subject of the final two chapters: Chapter 6 asks whether Star Wars will work; Chapter 7 looks at the strategic implications of SDI, and the arguments for and against Canadian participation. Finally, a conclusion sets out some alternatives for Canadian policies on the arms race.

1
Genesis of a Missile

The basic concept of the Cruise missile is not new: a guided, unmanned missile which (unlike a ballistic missile) is not propelled by an explosion, but cruises like a plane on wings. The idea dates back to World War I, when the U.S. army designed the "Bug," a gyro-guided, papier-mâché airplane that could deposit a 300-pound warhead thirty-five miles away. The Great War ended before the Bug could be used, but during World War II the Germans developed the first real Cruise missile, the V-1 "Buzz Bomb" or "Doodlebug." This missile was fired from launching strips in Northern France and Belgium and had a range of about 100 miles. It carried a high explosive (non-nuclear) warhead and was extremely inaccurate. It could, however, be fired in broad daylight when it was too dangerous for manned bomber missions.

In spite of its inaccuracy, the V-1 was at first quite effective. But because the technology was crude — the missile was large, slow and flew at a relatively high altitude — English air defenses were able to adapt. Royal Air Force pilots developed the skill of flying alongside a German V-1 and redirecting it with the wings of their aircraft so that the missile flew harmlessly out to sea. For the remainder of the war, the "Buzz Bomb" was more a nuisance than a threat.

Nuclear-armed Cruise missiles entered the arsenals of the United States and the USSR in the 1950s. The

U.S. produced a number of different types. The Navy was outfitted with the Regulus Cruise missile, which could be fired from the decks of submarines, aircraft carriers and cruisers. Ground-launched Matadors and later Mace Cruise missiles were based by the United States in West Germany. In 1959 the United States, in response to a non-existent "bomber gap," fielded the "Hound Dog" Cruise missile, a "stand-off" defense suppression weapon (i.e., a missile for knocking out anti-aircraft batteries) which could be fired from beyond the reach of Soviet defenses. In 1961 the U.S. also deployed the "Quail," an unarmed decoy Cruise missile which emitted a radar signature just like that of a B-52 bomber.

A major problem with these early Cruise missiles was poor accuracy. Like ballistic missiles, the Cruise relies on inertial sensors to guide it to its targets. But because the early Cruise missiles took much longer to reach a target, small errors in position were more likely to accumulate. Slower than the speed of sound, the Cruise missiles were therefore subject to wind and weather. As a result, it was a stroke of luck if they hit the right city, much less the right factory or air field. The U.S. Air Force's intercontinental Cruise, the Snark, was absurdly inaccurate. In 1983 a Snark was found in the Brazilian jungle, where it had strayed over 1,000 miles off course twenty-five years earlier.

In addition, the early American Cruise missiles, like the V-1, were vulnerable to air defenses: they were large, slow, maintained a level flight, and could not take evasive manoeuvres.

The Soviet Union also had a series of air- and sea-launched Cruise missiles in the 1950s, all of which suffered from the same defects as the Americans'. In addition, they were short-ranged, thanks to inefficient

24 Misguided Missiles

engines. By the early 1960s it was clear to the Americans that ballistic missiles were much more reliable and cost-effective, and the U.S. abandoned the development of Cruise missiles for about ten years. During the 1960s the U.S. withdrew its Regulus, Matador and Mace Cruise missiles from Europe and mothballed the Snark.

The Soviets, however, were not ready to abandon Cruise missiles. In particular, as they lacked experience with aircraft carriers, they developed and deployed a series of short-range submarine-based and surface ship-based Cruise missiles to provide fleet support. Similarly, for short-range naval and ground force support, the Russians developed air-borne Cruise missiles.

When in 1967 the Egyptians sunk the Israeli destroyer *Elath* with the Soviet SS-N-2 sea-launched non-nuclear Cruise missile, the U.S. was prompted to reinstitute development of the Cruise missile in the form of the short-range anti-ship "Harpoon." But the modern generation of the Cruise missile really got its big start in the late 1960s, when officials in the Pentagon's Office of Systems Analysis — the home of Defense Secretary Robert McNamara's famed "whiz kids" — needed something with which to fight off the Air Force's demands for a new intercontinental bomber to replace the aging B-52, which Air Force officers said would soon be unable to penetrate Soviet air defenses. The Air Force wanted an even bigger bomber, first a model called the B-70, then another known as the Advanced Manned Strategic Aircraft — both of which were predecessors of the current B-1. Systems analysts decided to put a lot of money into two alternative programs: the short-range attack missile (SRAM) and subsonic Cruise unarmed decoy (SCUD). The Hound Dog Cruise missile was swiftly and successfully turned into SRAM. The Air Force welcomed it, especially because it was short range (100 miles). The constant fear, which was later proved correct, was that too successful a long-range stand-off missile would threaten the whole rationale of the manned bomber itself. But the new decoy, SCUD, had to have greater range to be of any use at all, and therefore was potentially even more of a threat to the B-1 than the attack missile. Aside from the absence of a warhead, SCUD was much like the modern air-launched Cruise.

There were other analysts, however, notably the Pentagon's director of defense research and engineering, who questioned using a missile solely for the purpose of taking heat off penetrating B-52s. If the Air Force was going to the trouble of procuring a missile that had sufficient range and speed to confuse Soviet air defenses, why not give it some payload? Analysts soon proposed a warhead to ensure that the Russians would have to attack the missile even if they recognized it as a decoy, and SCUD became SCAD ("unarmed" became "armed"). Propelled by a turbofan engine (equipped by Litton Industries of California) and capable of a range of 1,000 miles, the decoy was beginning to look to the Air Force like a weapon that required little or no penetration of Soviet air space by a bomber. But the Air Force brass insisted throughout that this was a decoy and not a stand-off — let alone a long-range Cruise missile. Otherwise, the bomber would have nothing to do. It would have been as if a wooden duck had told the hunter to go home and get some breakfast.

SCAD was the immediate forebear of the modern Cruise missile. Intrigued by SCAD's technical possibilities, the Pentagon's Directorate of Defense Research and Engineering (DDRE) proposed that more advanced versions be developed — newer models with still longer range, better accuracy, and a nuclear warhead. The concept of a terrain-following guidance system had been around for years. In fact, such a system had been a feature of the Mace Cruise missile in the late 1950s — and had failed. DDRE thought that the addition of a computerized map would solve those early problems.

The revival of the Cruise missile in its current long-range form is the result of technological advances: satellites make accurate terrain maps of the Soviet Union possible; micro-circuits permit small guidance systems to take advantage of the terrain maps; miniaturization allows small but powerful nuclear weapons to take up little missile space (about three feet); and compact, highly efficient jet engines offer greater range and further savings on missile size. Other useful technological innovations that came to fruition in the early 1970s included small, efficient turbo-fan engines, missile frames that reflect less on radar screens, and solid-state electronics which make light, accurate guidance and control systems possible. Strategists soon found the Cruise much more attractive. What transformed a neglected missile into an important part of U.S. defense programs was a collection of rather uncoordinated technological innovations rather than a deliberate effort to develop a particular weapon for particular military missions.

The development of the modern Cruise missile began in June of 1972 when the U.S. Secretary of Defense Melvin Laird requested the appropriation of $20 million to develop Cruise missiles. The request was included in a group of amendments to the 1973 defense budget. At the time there was litle concrete evidence suggesting that long ranges could be drawn from so small a vehicle or that high accuracies could be achieved at the end of a two- or three-hour flight. Work focused immediately on the option of a submarine-launched Cruise missile and the first Navy test began in March of 1973. Within a year, it became apparent that Cruise missiles with terrain contour matching (TERCOM) navigation systems could theoretically achieve remarkably high accuracy — within 400 feet of a target. By the spring of 1974 the program evolved into planning for a new family of U.S. Cruise missiles ranging from strategic air-launched models to conventional anti-ship missiles. The Cruise missile was given its go-ahead during the Ford administration and was offered to an at first unenthusiastic military as solace for the Strategic Arms Limitation Talks (SALT I). It was also touted as a "bargaining chip" in negotiations with the Soviet Union. Additionally, and possibly most importantly, it appeared inexpensive. We'll examine each of these justifications in turn.

Rationale for the Cruise

In return for agreeing to support ratification of the SALT I Treaty (May 1972), the Joint Chiefs of Staff and Senate "hawks" extracted assurances from President Nixon that they would get an extensive nuclear weapons development and modernization program. The decision to proceed with the Cruise missile was a significant part of this pay-off to the Pentagon. Secretary of Defense Melvin Laird saw Cruise missiles as a legal way to evade the restrictive impact of the SALT agreement, as Cruise missiles were not part of the treaty restrictions. As one Soviet observer put it, "The Pentagon saw in this a loop-hole for circumventing SALT I and gaining unilateral advantages." Cruise missiles would be, as the Pentagon described them, "SALT-free," and were made to order for those in the White House and Pentagon frantically looking for ways of getting around the SALT I agreement. When Laird began looking for a suitable weapon system which could be built without violating the terms of Salt I (even while it was intended to violate the spirit), the Cruise was a natural since the Navy (or more exactly, one of the Navy divisions) had already been toying with the idea of a strategic Cruise missile. On the recommendation of the Pentagon and the Directorate of Defense Research and Engineering, Melvin Laird proposed the development of a submarine-launched long-range Cruise missile to the Senate Armed Services Committee.

There was nothing particularly new about subordinating arms control to the imperative of keeping ahead of the Soviets in the nuclear arms race. When it has come to a crunch between the pursuit of arms limitation and the demands of rearmament, all U.S. administrations have given priority to a military build-up. From the multiple independently targetable re-entry vehicle (MIRV) to the Strategic Defense Initiative, no American innovation in nuclear weaponry has been sacrificed on the altar of arms control. Thus, limits on ballistic missiles in SALT I generated both a military and political appetite for Cruise missiles.

The Cruise missile was seen by some White House and Pentagon officials as a bargaining chip — a new weapon system employed to gain leverage in future superpower arms bargaining. In justifying his Cruise missile proposal to the Senate Armed Services Committee, Defense Secretary Laird argued that the United States was able to negotiate effectively in SALT I because it had active development programs in the various areas of weaponry covered by the agreement. The United States had made an unsuccessful attempt to bring Soviet naval Cruise missiles into the SALT I accord and Laird felt that SALT II would produce the same results unless the U.S. launched a Cruise missile program of its own. Later in the same hearings he stated: "The development of the SLCM [sea-launched Cruise missile] is necessary to assure availability of future U.S. options for additional U.S. strength, if needed." This became known as the "Laird Hexahedge." It indicates that in 1972 Laird couldn't think of any specific reason why the weapons should be developed. Congress wasn't impressed and cleared only one-third of the requested funds. However, the program survived.

Many times during the 1970s Pentagon officials tried to entice reluctant members of Congress to appropriate more money for new weapons by emphasizing that bargaining chips were essential for success in the upcoming SALT II. In essence, they argued that more weapons were needed for arms control negotiations than were needed for military security itself. Negotiators spurred on Cruise development, sometimes against military resistance. The Cruise program might have foundered had it not been for the support of Secretary of State Henry Kissinger, who was looking for "marginal" systems that could be bargained away. Kissinger in particular saw the air-launched Cruise missile as a bargaining chip to trade away if the Soviet Union would agree not to produce mobile land-based missiles. U.S. officials calculated that such missiles would be more advantageous to the Soviet Union, given its greater land mass and internal secrecy, than they would be to the United States. Kissinger and civilian leaders in the Pentagon urged the military services to go ahead with the Cruise even though the military was not enthusiastic about its technical prospects. According to some sources, Kissinger practically forced the Cruise missile on the Navy and later the Air Force.

Unfortunately, it has always been the case that bargaining chips cannot necessarily be cashed in. Weapons initially justified as something to trade away soon become building blocks — weapon systems that are permanent parts of the arsenal. The nuclear arms race has been characterized by a tendency to rationalize weapon systems of otherwise dubious merit as bargaining chips, despite overwhelming evidence that such coercion almost always serves to toughen the adversary's bargaining position. The past thirty years of arms negotiations have demonstrated that U.S. resolve to expand its military prompts a renewed Soviet military build-up, not a mutually satisfactory agreement to reverse the build-up.

Probably the biggest selling point for the development of the modern Cruise missile was its price. One strategic analyst, John Foster, was so impressed with the potential of Cruise missiles that he ranked them ahead of the Trident missile and the B-1 bomber in cost effectiveness; the sea-launched Cruise missile, he said, "would add more deterrent per dollar than any other of our schemes." The Cruise was indeed seen as less expensive than any other kind of nuclear-weapon delivery system. Because the Cruise missile (unlike a manned bomber) was a one-shot deal expected to perform only once and for a few hours at most, certain short cuts could be made in design and production. Without a crew, there was no need for expensive safety devices in the engine, air frame and instrumentation. Cruise missiles became important because they seemed cheap. Otherwise, in all likelihood, reliance on ballistic missiles and bombers would have precluded their development.

The fiscal attractiveness of Cruise missiles would, of course, also not be lost on the Soviets. As one U.S. defense expert said, "If it's cheap for us, it's cheap for them." Reliable analysis of the cost effectiveness of the Cruise has, in fact, always been difficult to get. Cruise missiles do not seem so cheap when production costs rise — as always happens in military contracting — and when the associated costs such as the delivery system are added to the ledger.

The Military

The most curious aspect of Cruise missile history is that none of the three services (Air Force, Army and Navy) welcomed the weapon or sponsored its development. Service support for the weapon was limited, conditional or non-existent. The long-range air-launched Cruise missile (ALCM) was rammed down the throat of the Air Force. As we've seen, Air Force officers opposed the Cruise missile because it was being promoted as the substitute for new penetrating bombers and the existing SCAD program. In attempting to promote the B-1 bomber, Air Force generals stressed that an ALCM would, in their judgment, probably be vulnerable to terminal Soviet surface-to-air missile defenses. Additionally, they argued that relative to the B-1 the ALCM was not cost effective. The Air Force eventually accepted the long-range ALCM because the president ordered it to do so.

White House pressure in the mid-1970s forced the development of a ground-launched version of the Cruise missile. Its main virtues were always political: it was to be a SALT II bargaining chip and a highly visible symbol of America's commitment to Chancellor Schmidt's vision of Europe (see Chapter 4). The Army successfully fought having to accept the GLCM, arguing that priority had to be placed on rebuilding the Army after Vietnam and on refurbishing America's ground forces in Europe. As the Army refused to accept development responsibility for the GLCM, in 1979 the Air Force got stuck with it. This branch of the forces viewed the GLCMs as a "national mission" — one it performed for the country but that had little value for its own missions. Being compelled to accept the overgrown decoy was a bitter pill for the Air Force to swallow; not only did the decoy seem to have killed the Air Force's cherished bomber, but it didn't even have a pilot! Not surprisingly, the GLCM was given low priority during the annual budget negotiations with the secretary of defense.

Cruise enthusiasts might have expected the welcome to be a bit warmer in the Navy. If flexibility and versatility are the ideal qualities of a general purpose weapon system, the Tomahawk Cruise missile might seem the answer to an admiral's prayer. It has a long reach and a large payload, it can be nuclear or conventionally armed, it can be used against ships at sea and targets on land, it can be fitted aboard surface ships and submarines, and it can be emplaced ashore or carried by aircraft. On first impression it appears to be a universal weapon, and it has even been suggested that it will revolutionize naval warfare.

However, Navy experience with Cruise missiles in the 1950s had been unsatisfactory and did not favourably dispose officers to the modern Cruise missile. But while the Air Force and Army have a relatively tight hierarchical structure, the Navy has long been more decentralized into three autonomous factions: the surface fleet, the carrier fleet and the underwater fleet. This structure shaped much of the politics of Cruise missile development within the Navy because it gave naval Cruise missile proponents more freedom to manoeuvre than their Army counterparts.

The sea-launched Cruise missile (SLCM) has been a weapon in search of a mission. The submarine division liked land-attack SLCMs in principle but opposed them because of the competition for dollars and the likelihood that Cruise missiles would be installed primarily at the expense of the torpedo inventory, which would detract from the Navy's primary anti-submarine warfare role. To fire the SLCM at a target deep in the Soviet Union, moreover, would entail moving the attack submarines in toward enemy coastlines, thereby increasing the risk of detection. The firing of an SLCM would generate bubbles and acoustic signals that could reveal the submarine's location. In addition, because guidance alignment would require at least twenty minutes after the missile was loaded in a torpedo tube, a submarine could fire only infrequent salvos even while assuming high risks of detection.

Adding Cruise missiles to surface ships for land-attack missions would constrain their operational flexibility by requiring them to operate within range of the intended target. Long sea passages, possibly through contested waters, might be required to reach their designated launch positions. Designating general purpose ships for support in a land war would deplete forces committed to the Navy's primary role: control of communication by sea lines. As Rear Adm. Powell Carter, then director of strategic and theatre warfare, testified, "From the standpoint of military effectiveness, putting Cruise missiles on our general purpose forces is not a very wise thing to do."

The sinking of the *Elath* with Soviet surface-to-surface Styx anti-ship Cruise missiles had much impressed the surface fleet admirals. But the influential carrier admirals were hostile to the short-range anti-ship Cruise missile (TASM) because it represented a clear and present danger to the mission of the carrier-based aircraft. The TASM was the only version of the SLCM that a powerful sub-group within any of the services enthusiastically desired, and the surface fleet had to proceed cautiously and indirectly to get it. Few in the Navy were motivated strongly enough to work for the cancellation of the SLCM and many outside pushed hard in its favour. The Navy's sole interest in an anti-ship Cruise missile was, to its displeasure, subordinated by the Pentagon to the long-range SLCM.

Without exception, the military services did not want long-range Cruise missiles if they threatened their respective dominant missions or ate into their scarce funds, and generally the Cruise did both. Through the 1970s the Pentagon's push for Cruise missiles came from the office of the secretary of defense rather than the military.

The Civilians

Why then did the U.S. develop Cruise missiles when none of the services wanted them? One possible answer is that technological innovations create an irresistible force in the arms race. As Samuel P. Huntington, the influential conservative political scientist, once said, it may be that "What is technically possible tends to become politically necessary." The Cruise missile engendered great enthusiasm because it was a classic application of what the great nuclear scientist Robert Oppenheimer called "sweet" technology. Sweet technologies like the Cruise missile are translated into development programs and end up as major weapon systems without any prior clear definition of need for such weapons, or even a clear perception of the missions that such weapons could perform. Technical innovation, however, is not sufficient to guarantee the development and deployment of any individual weapon. The Cruise missile would not have proceeded as fast and as far, or proceeded at all, had it not been for the intervention and support of high-level figures in the Pentagon, the White House and even the U.S. Department of State.

Civilian planners in the Pentagon were the most important promoters of the Cruise missile. In 1974 the Pentagon was directed by Congress to review the requirement for strategic Cruise missiles thoroughly. The program progressed well and by 1976 the Cruise missile had support from people in the Pentagon who saw it as cheap, SALT-free and a versatile weapon that would allow the U.S. strategic arsenal to be expanded. The versatility of the Cruise missile lent it an aura of being an easy, all-purpose answer for strategic and tactical requirements. For example, planners speculated that the Tomahawk Cruise missile might be capable of missions ranging from destroying a Soviet intercontinental ballistic missile silo with a nuclear warhead to cratering a runway in Angola with conventional ordnance.

Civilian enthusiasts in the Pentagon believed that the Cruise missile would be militarily good for everything. It was looked upon as a weapon for all seasons precisely because it had no clearly defined mission: it could serve as an addition to U.S. strategic intercontinental nuclear forces for those who were pressing for nuclear superiority, could serve as a SALT bargaining chip, and could be useful to those wishing to see modernization of NATO's long-range theatre nuclear forces. The Pentagon pushed Cruise missiles when service preferences appeared to stand in its way, because the Cruise missile promised to expand U.S. deliverable warheads at the fastest rate and least cost — an appealing combination for cost-conscious defense secretaries, budget directors and presidents. By 1976, when Henry Kissinger was trying to reach a new arms control agreement, the Pentagon was reluctant to give up the Cruise and it was off-limits as a bargaining chip. "Henry sold Cruise missiles to the Pentagon, and then he couldn't buy them back," recalls one official of the Ford era. Kissinger himself remarked, "I didn't realize the Pentagon would fall in love with Cruise missiles."

In fact Kissinger's attitude toward the Cruise missile remains unclear. Some maintain that he never intended to trade away the Cruise, particularly the ALCM, but only to use it to extract concessions from the Soviet Union because he accepted the prevailing view that it would assist in preserving a mixed force of "penetrators" and stand-off bombers. In any case, Washington began to think it could reap significant advantage from developing the Cruise. The bargaining chip was taken off the table. In January of 1977, Malcolm R. Currie, the Defense Department's director of research and engineering, commented confidentially in his annual report that "The advent of long-range, highly accurate Cruise missiles is perhaps the significant weapon development of the decade."

Another Pentagon rationale for Cruise development was to strain Soviet military resources by forcing the Soviets into a costly upgrading of their defenses. It has been estimated, for example, that the threat created by 1,000 Cruise missiles could force the Soviet Union to establish a ring of specialized radar and surface-to-air missiles around the whole of its territory, which could cost more than $30 billion. A fleet of 50 to 100 air-borne down-looking radar aircraft with an infrared (heat-sensitive) capability might cost a further $10 billion, and there would still be a need for manned interceptors to fill gaps in the system. A reliable defense against Cruise missiles would cause the Soviet Union to divert attention and resources from other military efforts. If the Russians were not spending these vast sums to counter the Cruise, they would be allocating them in large part to offensive systems targeted against Western Europe and North America. In the words of the U.S. under-secretary of defense for research and development, James Wade, "A massive air defense program such as they would need would be a hundred-billion dollar plus program and they wouldn't be able to put that money on the anti-submarine warfare problem they have."

But the Soviet Union will not be the only country confronting this problem after it develops its own long-range Cruise missiles. It has not yet been estimated what the cost to the United States will be when the Soviets inevitably match the American Cruise missile program. Recognizing this, the Air Force has already requested a $7.8-billion air defense build-up, comprising distant early warning (DEW-Line) radar upgrading and large purchases of AWACS (air-borne warning and control system) planes and F-15 interceptors. Just to attain a modest defense against Soviet Cruise missiles, the United States would need more than 2,400 interceptor aircraft, 4,400 surface-to-air missiles, and much expanded radar and communication systems, at a total cost of more than $1,000 billion. It remains to be seen whether the Canadian north will play a major role in Cruise missile interception (see Chapter 5).

Despite forces in the missile's favour, the rationale for the Cruise was still shadowy at the end of the Nixon-Ford era. It was at once an urgent strategic requirement and, according to the 1977 Authorization for Military Procurement hearings, a "hedge against the development of effective threats to pre-launch survivability of land-based forces, to in-flight vulnerability of ballistic missiles and to bomber survivability." In short, confusion still surrounded the need for the Cruise missile and what its military mission would be. Full commitment was far from secure.

Politics: Domestic and International

Political considerations provided the final launching pad for the Cruise missile. As the Brookings Institution concluded in its historical study of the Cruise missile: "The final word on the broad politics of Cruise missile development in the '70s is this: had it not been for politics, the Cruise missile in all its present versions might never have existed." In the SALT II negotiations the Cruise's role significantly changed from bargaining chip to political lubricant.

The Carter administration, which came to power in 1977, was largely opposed to the development of the Cruise missile because its small size was thought to be an insurmountable obstacle to the verification of compliance with potential arms limitations. However, President Carter soon found himself expressing support for the Cruise missile in order to placate Cold-War senators and build support for SALT II ratification. The administration's resistance was further worn down by European threats to withhold support for the SALT

II Treaty, then in the final stages of negotiation, unless modernization of intermediate nuclear weapons was forthcoming. Considerable concern was being expressed by NATO's European members about the credibility of the American nuclear umbrella in Europe in an era of strategic nuclear parity between the superpowers. The Europeans, led by Helmut Schmidt, were worried that the question of their security was being decided behind their backs. The Cruise missile negotiations were a special source of concern.

The Carter decision to deploy ground-launched Cruise missiles in Europe should not, however, be understood as a direct response to a European request. The Cruise missile in Europe will be discussed extensively in Chapter 4; here it suffices to point out that early in 1976, before the European governments are alleged to have "asked" for them, Cruise missiles had already been classified as a theatre (i.e., intermediate-range) nuclear weapon system. In January of 1977, U.S. Deputy Secretary of Defense Richard Clements ordered the development of a GLCM. This was enthusiastically supported by NATO's supreme allied commander for Europe. The GLCM's range was too short to hit anywhere except Canada or Latin America from the United States, so where else could GLCMs be based but Europe? Clearly, the GLCM program was begun before any "need" for the weapon had been articulated, and many months before NATO's High Level Group, which was to define that "need" formally, had even been convened. None of this is to say that increased European concern over perceived imbalances in the European nuclear theatre was not a sort of straw that broke the camel's back, guaranteeing European deployment of the Cruise missile. But the story is not simply one of a request and its fulfillment.

40 Misguided Missiles

In June of 1977, the Cruise missile program was given the decisive push it needed to enter the "big league." President Carter cancelled the Air Force's B-1 bomber, and to compensate proclaimed the long-range ALCM program a national priority. The president had built up a strong political investment in opposing production of the B-1 and perhaps also a deep dislike of it. But the Air Force and aerospace industry could not be left empty-handed. As one participant put it: "The existence of the B-1 made the Cruise missile option feasible." Authorization was given for the production of thousands of Cruise missiles to be carried by B-52 bombers. While continuing with their campaign for the B-1 (which they finally won after President Reagan was elected), the Air Force moved over to full support of the ALCM. The enormous funds that were available attracted great interest from giant commercial concerns such as Boeing and General Dynamics, and created the large bureaucratic structure that has carried the Cruise missile program forward. In a 1980 feature story, *Time* profiled the U.S. Cruise missile program, describing the fierce corporate competition at the end of the 1970s for lucrative Cruise missile construction contracts and a share in what the magazine called "The Aerospace business bonanza." The hard-sell attitude of the weapons manufacturers is well illustrated by this quote from a *Boston Globe* column in the business section written by Michael Johnson, a stockbroker and international relations specialist at Thomson McKinnon Securities Inc. in Boston:

> Cruise missiles, in a sea and air version, will be bought in quantities. They are a truly elegant solution, typical of what America can do if it so desires. If fired from

the Sears Tower in Chicago with the pitching mound of Yankee Stadium as a target, the Cruise missile would be considered to have missed if it hit home plate! Best bet is to buy the electronic technology which permits this revolutionary accuracy.

Between 1977 and 1979 many "liberal" groups were high on the value of the strategic ALCM since it was the main tool to fight off the Air Force's claim that it needed to build the B-1 bomber. The Cruise missile, being a "stand-off" weapon, would impart survivability to the U.S. bomber force which otherwise might become vulnerable to Soviet air defenses. The Carter administration preferred the Cruise to the B-1 because the White House had more confidence in the effect that the low detectability of the Cruise missile would have on Soviet radar than in the effect that the B-1 radar countermeasures would have had. When Defense Secretary Harold Brown presented his first annual report in February of 1978, the ALCM was described as "our highest national priority." Zbigniew Brzezinski, Carter's national security advisor, put the case for the ALCM as follows: "As head of the Soviet air defense I should prefer to defend the Soviet Union, by the middle or end of the 1990s, with the permanent air defense system in use against one hundred still very modern jets like the B-1 than against 5,000 Cruise missiles that could penetrate the air defense system like a swarm of bees."

Following Reagan's election there was considerable anti-Cruise sentiment in the U.S. Congress. The SLCM in particular was unpopular. The Reagan administration's response to these pressures was to say that it needed the weapons in order to exert leverage on the Soviets in arms talks. (Or as arms negotiator Paul Nitze put it in pleading with one senator who was threatening to withhold support for the Cruise missile program, the U.S. needed "negotiating wampum.") Suddenly the weapons were being defended as less important to the cause of rearmament than to the cause of arms control. But the case was a difficult one to make as Reagan was not seen to be bargaining in good faith with the Soviets.

In reality, precisely because Cruise missiles represented an area of American technological superiority and therefore potential military advantage, the Department of Defense would do everything it could to prevent the State Department from trading them away. The Joint Chiefs of Staff took the view that the SLCMs were, as weapons to use against Soviet ships and to "project power ashore," too valuable to lose. GLCMs were key to the deployment program in Europe and the Pentagon civilian officials held out against even the very lenient limits on ALCMs contained in SALT II.

The Rise of a Weapon

The genesis of the modern Cruise missile was rather disorderly. As a history teacher used to say about Rome's decline, the reasons were many and varied. Originally none of the military services, with the partial exception of the Navy, wanted it. However, limits on ballistic missiles in SALT I generated both a military and diplomatic appetite for Cruise missiles which became difficult to limit in SALT II. The Pentagon became reluctant to accept limits on a technology in which it had begun to develop a significant lead over the Russians. There was no pre-existing doctrinal requirement to prompt the Cruise's development; it was the *availability* of the technology that prompted its promotion. The Cruise programs evolved because of technology aided by timely intervention from civilian planners, not because the professional military believed they were necessary. The services for the most part resisted Cruise missiles for fear that they might mean reduced commitment to other, preferred weapon systems. Development was pushed by civilian technical specialists, systems analysts and managers. The result was that major changes in force structure were being made before the role of the weapons in the military operational doctrine had been fully articulated.

At every crucial stage in the development of each type of Cruise missile, high-level political intervention was necessary either to start it or to sustain it. All three versions of the Cruise have received decisive support from civilian officials in the Pentagon and senior decision-makers in the U.S. government. First the missiles were used as bargaining chips with which to wrest concessions from the Russians; second, as political lubricants with which to gain the acceptance of a SALT II accord by Congress and the NATO allies; and third, as significant military options to be protected in their own right because of their presumed enhancement of America's strategic retaliatory forces. Thus the Cruise missile program has reached its present stage by a mixture of political "pull," prolonged inter-service and intra-service skirmishing, and the momentum generated by the manufacturers' "push." As a result, the missile has at various times been all things to all men: a low-level decoy, an anti-ship missile and a tactical weapon. It was a curious and complex grouping of factors that converted the technologically possible into the politically necessary.

2
The Cruise: Capabilities and Arms Control

The Cruise missile is a small (2.5 feet wide and less than 20 feet long) and comparatively uncomplicated weapon system, but its consequences are likely to be large and complex. Essentially a small pilotless airplane carrying either a conventional or nuclear warhead, the Cruise is a self-guided weapon system that is powered by an air-breathing engine. This means that it must be continuously powered as it flies through the atmosphere — and that it is limited to relatively low speeds (approximately 500 miles per hour). In contrast, a ballistic missile (i.e., a rocket) is only powered for the first few minutes of its flight. After that it travels at speeds of between 5,000 and 10,000 miles per hour out into space on a trajectory which is determined by gravity and by the missile's position and velocity at the end of the powered portion of its flight. Several minutes later it re-enters the atmosphere to reach its target.

The Cruise missile has an on-board guidance system to keep it on course. It flies at a low altitude — less than 200 feet — tracing a meandering and deceptive course to elude enemy radar and penetrate defenses. Its low flight altitude makes its detection quite problematic because the nap of the earth limits the coverage of ground-based radar.

Capabilities and Arms Control 45

Critics have warned that Cruise missiles, like the neutron bomb, could lower the nuclear threshold and make nuclear war "more thinkable" because they are psychologically less forbidding than large nuclear weapons. But a Cruise missile has the explosive equivalent of 300,000 tons of TNT, or fifteen times the power of the Hiroshima or Nagasaki bomb. That is enough to knock out a city of 1,000,000 people. The United States plans to build approximately 5,000 of these 200 kiloton missiles, which amounts to a total of 1,000 megatons or the equivalent of 165 second world wars.

Five types of Cruise missiles are in the works: the air-launched Cruise missile (ALCM), the ground-launched version (GLCM) and three ship-launched or submarine-launched models (SLCMs). The ground-based Cruise missiles are known in the trade as "Glickems" and the sea-based as "Slickems." We'll examine the three varieties in turn.

The *air-launched Cruise missile* is a key component of the U.S. modernization program for strategic forces. Initially, B-52 bombers will carry six ALCMs on each of two winged pylons, retaining nuclear gravity bombs and short-range attack missiles in the internal bomb bay. In this first phase the bombers will operate in a "shoot and penetrate" mode, launching ALCMs from beyond Soviet defenses — the missiles have a range of 1,500 miles — and then flying on to use their other weapons. After late 1985 these bombers will be converted fully to Cruise missile carriers with internal rotary launcher racks. The American plan is to arm a total of 99 B-52s with 12 air-launched Cruise missiles each by 1986, at which time 96 B-52s will be equipped with internal rotary launchers to carry a total of 20 each. The Reagan administration's plans also call for the deployment of as many as 30 ALCMs on 100 B-1 bombers. The first full squadron of ALCMs on B-52 long-range bombers — stationed at Griffiss Air Force Base in Rome, New York (about 90 miles southeast of Kingston, Ontario) — became operational in December of 1982.

Four hundred and sixty-four *ground-launched Cruise missiles* are scheduled for deployment in Western Europe as part of NATO's controversial modernization and expansion of its longer-range nuclear forces (the GLCMs have a range of 1,300 to 1,500 miles). These deployments in five Western European countries are underway. The GLCMs are able to be mobile in groups of sixteen missiles. Four weapons will be carried on each transporter-erector-launcher (TEL) in a convoy of vehicles with launch centres and other support elements. The TEL enables the GLCM to be mobile and therefore less vulnerable to attack. During full-alert periods the GLCM units would disperse to "satellite stations."

Sea-launched Cruise missiles represent the Pentagon's most ambitious Cruise program. Of the three models, two are conventionally armed: the tactical anti-ship missile (TASM) and one model of the Tomahawk missile (TLAM-C, the "C" denoting conventional). Both of these have modest ranges: 300 and 700 miles respectively.

The Tomahawk land-attack missile nuclear armed (TLAM-N) can be fired from torpedo tubes. Its range is similar to the GLCM's. Once the missile clears the surface of the water, the wings and air-intake pop out and the missile takes off with its own jet engine. Therefore, ordinary cruisers, battleships, destroyers and hunter-killer submarines can be transformed into delivery platforms for strategic nuclear weapons, and the enemy will have little or no idea of which submarine the missiles are deployed on. Current Reagan administration plans call for approximately 1,000 nuclear armed SLCMs. After 1986, the United States Navy will begin using a vertical launch system which will be fitted to both surface ships and attack submarines in order to conserve torpedo tube space and to increase nuclear weapons capacity. According to Navy plans, the nuclear-armed SLCMs are to be used as a "strategic reserve." In the event of a nuclear war lasting over several weeks or months, nuclear SLCMs would be used to strike military and civilian targets that remained after the initial nuclear exchange. As well as being "useful" as part of a massive nuclear attack on the USSR, it has been suggested that SLCMs could play an important part in a naval battle, destroying ports and Soviet naval air facilities. The second suggestion involves the dubious proposition that a "theatre" naval nuclear war could be fought without escalating to all-out nuclear war. As we'll see in Chapter 3, the Pentagon may well have even more aggressive and provocative purposes for the SLCM.

The TERCOM Guidance System

The critical part of long-range Cruise technology lies in the missile's specially developed guidance mechanisms. The considerable accuracy of these new Cruise missiles is provided by a "terrain contour matching" system (TERCOM), manufactured in part by Litton Industries in Rexdale, Ontario. An on-board computer has a "picture" of the terrain over which the missile is programmed to fly, and during flight uses a radar altimeter to "see" the surface of the terrain below. In this system, sections of the flight path to the target are surveyed in advance by satellite in order to determine variations in ground level. These surveyed areas are divided into a matrix of squares and each square is given a number representing the average elevation of the ground (a high number for a hill, a low number for a valley). At pre-set intervals the computer compares the terrain's features with a pre-programmed map (up to thirty maps of areas en route to the target can be stored). The computer then adjusts the missile's flight path to coincide with the pre-set course. Between TERCOM updates, an inertial guidance system based on a package of accelerometers and gyroscopes keeps the missile on course. As it approaches its target, radar in the nose of the missile compares the target area with its computer memory. This enables the Cruise to "home in" on its target. With this system, Cruise missiles can theoretically arrive within 100 yards (possibly as close as 30 yards) of their targets after a 1,500-mile flight. At their best, Cruise missiles are two and a half times as accurate as the MX. Designers say their computer system is so advanced that a Cruise missile can be programmed to go through the front door of its target (house-address accuracy!). Needing absolute precision to compensate for smaller explosive yields, conventionally-armed Cruise missiles are additionally equipped with a digital scene-matching area correlator in order to lock the missile in on its target during the final approach.

The extremely high accuracy of Cruise missiles is a significant development. This accuracy enables them to score practically direct hits on their chosen targets and to destroy enemy missiles, even in hardened concrete silos. However, because the missiles would take two hours or more to reach targets, they are aimed, for the most part, at fixed enemy installations such as air defense centres, nuclear storage areas and command and control posts. The TERCOM guidance system enables the missile to fly at tree-top level following a zig-zag course, which minimizes radar detection and makes it difficult to knock down. In this way, the range in which the missile can be detected by ground-based radar is greatly reduced and the course can be programmed to avoid known radar bases or to take advantage of ground obstructions. The Cruise has a radar image of about the size of a seagull and may be made even smaller by further changes in design.

These capabilities are, of course, theoretical. Short of actual use in war only testing can verify whether or not the weapon lives up to its promise. And some experts are not particularly high on the Cruise. Dina Rasor, director of the Project on Military Procurement, is blunt: "The concept [of the Cruise missile] may sound wonderful — arms control groups talk about how deadly and awful it is — but when you really come right down and look at it, there are some serious problems with whether it works or not." According to the Boeing Corporation, however, the air-launched Cruise missile has "passed every test thrown at it with flying colours."

But a manufacturer is not usually the most reliable judge of a product's reliability. A 1980 report for the U.S. General Accounting Office, the watchdog arm of Congress, revealed that the missile's engine often wouldn't start when cold. Work on a special ignition system to solve the starting problem was cancelled because of rising costs. In the early stages of modern Cruise development, several missiles crashed or flew off course. Indeed, only two-thirds of the first thirty Cruise missile tests were successful and even that figure is liberal, since tests in which the missiles literally didn't get off the ground were not included. The *Wall Street Journal* reported on the failure of two (out of two) operational flight tests of the Cruise missile: "The Air Force doesn't call the tests 'failures,' preferring to call them 'partial successes' because the missiles worked 'flawlessly' until they went off course." The U.S. Air Force points to eight consecutive successful 1983 Cruise tests as evidence that Cruise missiles do work, but it sometimes concedes that the missiles hardly function perfectly. At the end of 1982 it was reported that the U.S. government had to set up a special team to iron out some problems associated with TERCOM, primarily because the guidance system could not prevent the missile from flying into power cables. A June 1983 report released by the General Accounting Office said that both ALCMs and GLCMs are being deployed without sufficient testing. Cruise testing in northwest Canada during 1984 and 1985 has been more successful than earlier trial runs, but it is still far from certain if all the problems have been worked out.

Even when testing is successful, major problems persist. Much of the Cruise testing has been unrealistic, as most of the test flights have been carried out in the southwest of the United States where the terrain is hilly, without much vegetation, and very thoroughly mapped, providing ideal conditions for TERCOM. Over the very flat terrain of much of the USSR, however, TERCOM would have more difficulty, particularly as it is much harder to obtain sufficiently accurate (to within ten feet) altitude maps. The TERCOM guidance update system is of no use over flat land. Because one square mile looks more or less the same as the next, TERCOM — which relies on distinguishable differences in terrain — would not know where it was. One Pentagon official who helped to direct the Cruise missile program admits that "There are certain areas of the Soviet Union that are like a billiard table, and TERCOM won't work there." This limitation would be especially significant because the flattest and most featureless areas of the USSR are along the northern steppes. This is precisely the part of the country that the ALCMs would have to traverse immediately after being launched from a B-52 or B-1 bomber (which would carry them to just outside Soviet air-space). If the missile went off track at the beginning of the journey, the errors would become cumulative and finally the missile would get lost. A designer of guided missiles formerly with one of the military's leading test facilities explains: "TERCOM is like a very narrow road map. If you get off into another country you don't know where you are any more." (Ground-launched and sea-launched Cruise missiles would be less subject to this limitation since they could approach their targets from the east or west.) Moreover, according to a 1980 report by the General Accounting Office, the Defense Mapping Agency "overestimated its capacity to produce digital maps for the TERCOM's use." The stringent accuracy requirements of the Cruise missile may also demand more precise maps of the Soviet Union than can be obtained through satellite photography. Even in test flights over the United States the Air Force's test centre has had to admit that map errors mean that the missiles "frequently crash into tall obstacles on their way to their targets." The ability of U.S. aircraft to take more precise aerial pictures while flying over Soviet routes is, of course, rather limited.

Another major difficulty is the problem of "seasonal variation." During the average period of 120 days a year that northern Russia is covered with snow, and during warm weather periods when trees have heavy foliage, would the radar altimeter take misleading readings? Snow-drifts and the leaves of forest trees could produce reflections of the radar that the missile uses to gauge its height. Consequently, the contours that the missile would see might be different from the contours on its built-in maps, prepared earlier and possibly during a different season. If this is so, then the missile would simply lose its way. McDonnell Douglas, which designs TERCOM, claims that this is not a problem, but critics are skeptical. In addition, some snow-covered Arctic terrain has few recognizable features for the missile to follow on a flight into the Soviet Union. The General Accounting Office report made some other points. Because the Cruise engine isn't sufficiently powerful at present, the missile often can't react quickly enough to changes in the altitude of the ground and so tends to crash into ridges. It may become entangled in power lines and its small size makes it vulnerable to sudden gusts of wind. The report concludes: "Cruise missiles will work under specific conditions. However, if any of these conditions change, the accuracy of the missile could deteriorate rapidly."

In the middle and late 1970s, Cruise missiles were often hailed as probably unstoppable wonder weapons — the most dazzling display of military microcomputer technology the world had ever seen. The McDonnell Douglas Corporation promoted the Cruise missile as "a missile for all seasons: neither snow nor rain nor leaves nor gloom of night stays Cruise missiles from the swift completion of their appointed rounds."

It is very dangerous to believe all the claims that the U.S. military and the weapons contractors make about the capabilities of their weapons. In order to be funded by Congress, every new weapon has to be hailed as a great advance over the previous models. Only competitors refer to any defects. But even if testing problems were resolved, there would remain a tendency to over-rate the Cruise missile as an undetectable and unstoppable weapon. Neither the benefit nor the disadvantages of Cruise missiles are as revolutionary or as simple as either advocates or opponents originally believed.

Uses

The most basic criticism of the Cruise missile from the disarmament movement is that it has been designed as a "useable" part of a nuclear war-fighting strategy. This capability does not, however, make the Cruise a "first-strike" weapon if that term is used to mean a successful nuclear attack by one side against the other's nuclear weapon systems. A disarming first strike means a sudden mass attack aimed to destroy the opponent's nuclear missiles and bombers before they can be launched in retaliation. It also involves the destruction of at least the major command bunkers from which the enemy directs its nuclear forces and communications equipment such as early-warning satellites. No disarming first strike could ever be perfectly executed; the objective would be to destroy a sufficient proportion of an enemy's weapons to ensure that the damage that the remainder could inflict would be kept within "acceptable" limits (however "acceptable" might be defined).

Many in the Canadian disarmament movement still refer to the Cruise missile as a first-strike weapon. It is true, of course, that the launching of a Cruise missile is difficult to detect. When a ballistic missile is launched, satellites can detect the heat from the rocket.

But because the booster rocket of the ground- and sea-launched Cruise missile fires for only about twenty seconds before the turbo-fan engine takes over, and the air-launched Cruise missile uses no booster rocket at all, the USSR is unlikely to be able to detect a Cruise missile on launch. All other things being equal, this would give the Cruise a first-strike capability.

Yet to fulfill a first-strike mandate a nuclear weapon would not only have to be extremely accurate but also possess a short warning time between launch and impact. The Cruise missile is much too slow for such a duty. It would be foolish to attempt to initiate a first strike with Cruise missiles and run the risk that they would be detected during their relatively long flight time. Leonard Bertin of the International Institute of Strategic Studies makes this point quite clear: "No country which has an established ICBM system with a travel time of twenty minutes to strategic targets deep in enemy territory is going to prejudice that capability by risking the detection of Cruise missiles of relatively short range that take four hours to reach targets only 3,000 kilometres away." And these missiles would have been launched by aircraft that probably would have already shown up on radar screens. Additionally, the massive air-defense forces of the Soviet Union are already capable of shooting down at least some of the slow (about 450 miles per hour) Cruise missiles with missiles and guns. Soviet area defenses feature airborne warning and control systems (AWACS) and "look-down shoot-down fighters" with advanced missiles equipped with radar speakers which could reach out long distances from the Soviet borders to attack Cruise missile carriers before the missiles were launched. The Soviets are now deploying 11-76 mainstay aircraft which have capabilities similar to those of the American AWACS. These fly at 40,000 feet and should in theory be able to look down with their radar and spot a Cruise missile when it is about 250 miles away. Soviet terminal defenses feature the new SA-10, a high performance surface-to-air missile, along with radars having excellent subclutter visibility (necessary to identify small objects). The Russians are reportedly placing SA-10 radar atop tall steel towers. According to the former U.S. under-secretary of defense, William Perry, the SA-10 could "have a formidable capability against the Cruise missile."

The Soviet Union has already developed a lookdown shoot-down system for its Foxbat interceptor, which, according to a report in *Aviation Week*, has been tested successfully against drones simulating the Tomahawk Cruise. The Soviet Union is now developing a supersonic fighter to intercept and shoot down Cruise missiles. According to the authoritative magazine *Jane's Defence Weekly*, the four-engine aircraft may be able to carry as many as thirty air-to-air missiles. That many rockets would give the mystery jet, known in the West as Aircraft 101, the capacity to intercept waves of missiles. Aircraft 101 could deal with a massive assault by air- and ground-launched Cruise missiles, says the editor of *Jane's*, John R. Taylor.

The Soviet Union is also developing a new type of surface-to-air missile especially designed to shoot down Cruise missiles. The new surface-to-air missile is designed to pop up from its launcher and dive on the low-flying Cruise. Electronic countermeasures might also prove troublesome for the Cruise missile, critics suggest. Although the missile's altimeter looks straight down, some critics claim it has large sidelobes. Kosta Tsipis, a Massachusetts Institute of Technology physicist who once thought highly of the Cruise missile's technological prowess but who now detects flaws, says that "you can just beam from any direction and if the missile goes by it gets jammed. You can jam the missile with trivial effort."

In 1981 the American Army and Air Force jointly conducted tests pitting a drone simulating the Air Force ALCM against the Army's improved I-Hawk surface-to-air missile. Air Force officials have no comment on the results but analysts in the Pentagon and congressional staff say that the I-Hawk detected, tracked and could have shot down the Cruise missile in at least seven and possibly nine of ten engagements. After receiving the assessment of the Army Missile Intelligence Agency, Pentagon officials admitted privately that this model of ALCM was obsolete even before it went into service. U.S. Intelligence reports have indicated that in tests Soviet MIG-25s flying at 20,000 feet have successfully destroyed a number of target missiles flying at 1,000 feet or less. A far greater threat to Cruise missiles will emerge as Soviet look-down shoot-down radar and interceptor aircraft improve. These developments are hardly unexpected but have been used by the United States to justify the development of the improved "stealth" Cruise missile.

Consequently, the Cruise missile is a poor first-strike weapon for the United States. That fact, in turn, has several reassuring implications with regard to Moscow's strategic behaviour. Most notably, the Cruise missile (unlike the Pershing II, MX, etc.) does not further encourage the development of a Russian launch-on-warning posture. Because the Cruise missile is too slow to be effective as a tool for the pre-emptive destruction of Soviet land-based missiles, it does not add to the USSR's incentive to launch an initial intercontinental ballistic missile salvo in a "use them or lose them" predicament.

While not at present (or in the near future) a first-strike weapon, the Cruise is, however, a first-use weapon if we use the term to refer to nuclear weapon systems that are designed for intimidation and fighting nuclear war. The SLCMs, for example, are described by the U.S. Office of the Chief of Naval Operations as "additional survivable nuclear forces for the strategic reserve force" that "could be pivotal in the post-war balance and struggle for victory." The Cruise missile is deployed not only for the purpose of assured destruction but for the purpose of attacking secondary military targets such as air fields, naval facilities and so on. Such targets (being immobile) do not require instant destruction but they do require accuracy and lower-yield warheads to limit collateral damage (the theoretical point being that in a protracted nuclear war attacks must be limited to avoid triggering a massive Soviet response — this of course assumes that the Soviets have the capacity to distinguish between massive and limited nuclear attacks). In this scenario, the Cruise missile, used in very large numbers, would cross-target missile control centres and silos, air fields and other facilities, "mopping up" the nuclear weapons that had escaped the first strike by fast ballistic missiles. Specific guidance systems have been developed that would enhance this role. The most important is a system called Autonomous Terminal Homing (ATH) which should be available on Cruise missiles in the late 1980s. With ATH, sensors in the nose of the Cruise missile detect whether the target has already been hit by a nuclear weapon and, if so, would re-route the Cruise missile to a new target.

For strategic nuclear forces, Cruise missiles offer less than early enthusiasts hoped for or opponents concerned about arms control feared. But the Cruise has more significance than can be inferred from narrowly focusing on the weapon in isolation from other elements of force structure. The prestigious Stockholm International Peace Research Institute points out:

> The role of the Cruise missile in the strategic counterforce strategies of the USA and USSR is not yet clear. The relatively slow speed of the missile reduces its effectiveness as a surprise first-strike weapon. However, its ability to evade defensive radars, its relatively low cost, which allows for the stockpiling of large numbers, and above all its exceptionally high accuracy suggests that it is intended to play an important role in limited nuclear war. However, it would be premature to discount the full strategic counterforce implications of the long-range Cruise missile. The high accuracy and mobility of Cruise missiles and their ability to confuse and overwhelm defenses suggest that they could play an important role in a first strike if they could be launched reasonably close to their targets, and if their launching could be coordinated with strikes by long-range missiles in such a way as to bring them all to their targets within a relatively short time.

In Chapter 3, the increasing American priority on nuclear war-fighting in "limited nuclear wars" will be examined with particular reference to how the Cruise missile fits into the total U.S. nuclear strategy.

Generations of the Cruise

Richard Betts of the Brookings Institution has said: "Cruise missile policy is a bucket of worms. The weapons themselves have been continually changing.''

Indeed the modern Cruise missile — or what is called a second-generation Cruise — is a relatively new weapon and its performance can be substantially improved over time with respect to greater range and speed, lesser detectability, and the provision of electronic countermeasures, decoys and multiple warheads.

Due to the projected vulnerability of Cruise missiles to Soviet air defenses, the U.S. Air Force decided to end production of ALCMs in 1984 and began producing a newer version — a third-generation Cruise — called the Advanced Cruise Missile (ACM). The Pentagon, which once planned to buy as many as 4,800 ALCMs from Boeing, decided to end the program with a total inventory of only 1,715. Orders have been given to proceed with the construction of roughly 1,500 ACMs.

Very little is known about this new missile. The immediate priority seems to be on the upgrading of the current version with techniques such as radar-masking clutter and infra-red background — the technical name is "onboard electronic countermeasure systems." There is little doubt that "stealth" technology that makes the missile even harder to detect will be central to Cruise modernization. The stealth formula is a system of deceiving radar by electronically changing the reflected signal so that the radar operators don't see the intruding weapon. These advances in airframe shapes and material design will enhance the missile's ability to penetrate Soviet radar and air defenses. The missile will use materials (such as carbon fibre) that absorb rather than reflect radar signals. It will also have a smooth, low-angled shape, and engines with cooled exhaust to further minimize detection.

60 Misguided Missiles

While the idea behind stealth technology is relatively straightforward, the procedures necessary for pulling off radar invisibility are not easy to execute. Wolfgang Panofsky, director of Stanford University's Linear Excelerator Centre, is among those who believe that the Soviets have come up with "all sorts of tricks" to break the new stealth technology.

TERCOM is the Cruise guidance system for the immediate future only. ACMs will probably have some type of "digital scene-matching area correlator-type terminal homing device" which uses the ground's microwave (radar) reflectivity instead of its topography and, unlike the active TERCOM system, cannot be picked up by enemy radar. The ACMs will also be linked to the Navstar/Global Positioning System, a satellite navigational aid which will offer positional fixes of within about 50 feet when completed in 1988. A more comprehensive stand-off range of better than 2,000 miles will be achieved using higher-density fuel and "recuperative" engines which consume exhaust heat. One of the main reasons for shifting to an advanced or stealth Cruise missile is a hope that such missiles will be able to fly higher than the present Cruise without being detected. This would increase the missile's range and permit the Cruise to be launched farther from Soviet territory. Concerns that the current missiles are underpowered, causing them to crash when negotiating sudden obstacles, will be addressed by a more powerful engine. There can be little doubt that, in time, improved guidance systems, more efficient engines, on-board "threat detection" and manoeuvring capabilities will result in a speedier, more accurate, more destructive intercontinental-range Cruise missile.

Considerable effort is also being placed on speeding up the Cruise missile. McDonnell Douglas is developing a Cruise missile that is powered by a ram-jet engine. This missile is about six times faster than the present Cruise, but is less fuel-efficient, reducing its range to about 250 miles. In 1980 the U.S. Defense Advanced Research Projects Agency initiated a five-year Cruise program. Among the concepts studied was a supersonic Cruise missile which could penetrate enemy territory at altitudes above 100,000 feet while travelling many times the speed of sound. That would require a supersonic combustion ram-jet engine called a scramjet. It would most likely use liquid hydrogen, or what is known as "slurry" fuel. Later it might use a solid ram-jet fuel and, according to former Lockheed engineer Robert Aldridge, the development of "hard hydrogen" — a sort of hydrogen coal — seems to be a door-opener to that approach. The weight saved by eliminating fuel tanks, lines, valves and metering devices would increase the missile's effectiveness and range. The superadvanced Cruise missile is believed to be the size of an ALCM with a 2,600-mile range. It is thus quite possible that a later generation of the Cruise missile will achieve supersonic capabilities through advances in air-frame design, engine technology and fuel efficiency. Future developments in super-computers in the 1990s may also speed up the introduction of a supersonic Cruise missile.

Projecting further yet into the future, work is clearly being conducted on a fourth-generation Cruise missile. Dramatic improvements in the ratio of engine thrust to weight and in fuel efficiency, coupled with more modest increases in missile size, could well result in a weapon of intercontinental range and supersonic speeds. This would alter the nature of the Cruise missile radically. What was originally justified as a stabilizing system because it assured retaliation but was too slow for first-strike use might become a first-strike weapon which could attack any target in the Soviet Union from a profusion of easily hidden launchers based in the United States. With the new elements of enhanced range, speed and penetration afforded by such a Cruise it is also the perfect prescription for a first strike.

While the current Cruise may not yet encourage a Soviet launch-on-warning posture, the continuing modernization of the Cruise is virtually guaranteed to feed growing — and vastly under-rated — Soviet anxieties over the possibility of a surprise attack, further pressuring the nuclear hair-trigger and increasing the likelihood of unintentional nuclear war. And at the moment there is nothing standing in the way of third- and fourth-generation Cruise missiles being tested in Canada (see Chapter 5).

The Russian Cruise

So much attention has been focused on the American Cruise missile that many tend to forget that the Soviet Union also deploys Cruise missiles, albeit of lesser sophistication and capabilities. The Cruise missiles that the Soviets have deployed on bombers and submarines for many years are considered technically primitive, short-range (about 350 miles), relatively inaccurate and very large. In the 1960s, the Russians developed and deployed a series of submarine- and surface ship-based Cruise missiles to provide tactical offensive and defensive fleet support. These SLCM submarines had to surface to launch their missiles. Similarly, for the tactical support of naval and ground forces, the Soviet Union developed ALCMs. These were not given land-attack missions, as the Soviet Union placed almost total reliance on ballistic missiles for this purpose. In reply to a question about whether Soviet Cruise missile submarines had ever been deployed in a way that threatened the United States, Secretary of Defense Harold Brown stated in 1979: "They were before they had ballistic missile submarines. As soon as they got ballistic missile submarines they stopped doing this.... They are not nearly so good for the purpose."

In 1969 the United States proposed a freeze on submarine-launched Cruise missiles, which at that time only the Soviets kept in operation. The chief Soviet negotiator, intent on ridiculing U.S. concern, compared Cruise missiles to "prehistoric animals of the Triassic period." By the 1970s the USSR had in operation several hundred sea-borne launchers for Cruise missiles and several hundred naval and tactical air-to-surface Cruise missiles with operational ranges of up to a few hundred miles. The Soviet Union also adapted naval surface-to-surface Cruise missiles for land-based coastal defense, and for some years deployed with army field forces tactical ground-launched Cruise missiles adapted from a naval missile. Although some research and testing had been conducted, the Soviet Union had not developed or deployed strategic or long-range land-based or aircraft-borne Cruise missiles.

A former U.S. Space Department official described Soviet Cruise missiles of the 1970s as "old, clunky, big and inaccurate weapons which people laughed at," and in 1976 the Department of Defense judged that "there is no evidence as yet that the Soviets possess the solid-state computer technology and small-engine design skill to pursue over the near term a strategic Cruise missile development program."

By 1980, however, there was clear evidence that the Soviets were engaged in a concerted Cruise missile development program to match that of the United States.

The Soviet Navy had about forty-five nuclear-powered and twenty-three diesel-powered submarines carrying a total of about 450 Cruise missiles with operational ranges of up to about 370 miles. A giant new Soviet submarine (Oscar class) armed with anti-ship Cruise missiles was launched and several hundred naval aviation and long-range aviation bombers were equipped to launch air-to-surface Cruise missiles, also with operational ranges of up to about 370 miles and to be used principally for naval missions. The U.S. was still comfortably ahead of the Soviets and at the time an American White House official stated that the Soviet missile was "as big as a boxcar and has one common characteristic — it dives into the ground every hundred feet." Defense Secretary Brown still characterized Soviet Cruise missiles as "way behind" U.S. systems. The only exception to American supremacy was in regard to short-range anti-ship Cruise missiles; the Soviets had already deployed Cruise missiles possessing supersonic speed.

Consequently, during SALT II the Soviets unsuccessfully pressed for a ban on long-range Cruise missiles. The Americans held firm to protect a promising new weapon with which the United States was thought to have a lengthy technological lead — SALT II merely prohibited long-range Cruise missile deployment until the end of 1981. Meanwhile, the Soviets scrambled to perfect a weapon similar to the Americans' and in a very few years they have come much closer to bridging the Cruise missile gap.

In 1984 the Russians placed long-range Cruise missiles (model AS-X-15) on aircraft. Yankee-class Soviet submarines are being refitted to carry Cruise missiles (SS-NX-21) which are similar in range, speed and payload, if not accuracy, to the U.S. Tomahawk

Cruise missile. The SS-NX-21, which is small enough to be launched from the standard Russian torpedo tube, has an estimated range of 1,860 miles and incorporates a turbofan engine as well as a guidance system which resembles TERCOM but is somewhat less sophisticated. Soviet ground-launched Cruise missiles will be deployed late in 1985 or in 1986.

American Cruise technology (with its small efficient jet engines, small warheads with high yields, accurate navigation aids) is still six to eight years ahead of the Soviet Union's by various estimates. But the Soviets are on the threshold of breaking the monopoly on modern Cruise missiles and just as they broke the American monopoly on MIRVs, it is prudent to assume that over the course of the 1980s they will achieve some approximation of current American Cruise weapons even if they do not keep pace with technological elaboration. That achievement would be sufficient to enable the Soviets to exploit some fundamental non-technical advantages in any extended competition between deployments. As John Steinbruner of the Brookings Institution has noted, the United States and most of its major allies have a high concentration of targets near coastal areas which are easily approached from the open ocean or through seas controlled by the Soviet Navy. By contrast, the Soviet Union is essentially a land-locked country with strong naval defenses in its few sea approaches. Moreover, though it is a less enduring advantage, historically the Soviet Union has developed a much more extensive air-defense system. Ironically, an extended competition in Cruise missile deployment could work to the advantage of the Soviets even if they are not as adroit in the emerging technology.

The Cruise and the Future of Arms Control

As we have already seen, considerable controversy exists over exactly what dangers are posed by the development of the Cruise missile. Confusion also surrounds the question of the ability of the superpowers to monitor — the technical term is verify — the number of Cruise missiles deployed by the other side.

Many in the disarmament community now observe that the monitoring problems associated with Cruise missiles herald the beginning of the end for verifiable arms control. William Epstein, former director of disarmament for the United Nations, explains:

> There is no known way to verify the number and location of Cruise missiles ... and no practical hope of being able to do so in the future. The implications are terrifying. There can be no way of assuring compliance with any treaty for limitation or elimination and governments would therefore not enter such agreements.

Daniel Ellsberg, former strategic analyst for the Rand Corporation and consultant to the U.S. Department of Defense, is characteristically blunt: "It [the Cruise missile] is essentially a weapon against arms control." James Stark, past president of Operation Dismantle, is equally emphatic: "The Cruise missile, due to its small size, is unverifiable and I defy anyone to prove otherwise."

It is indeed true that because the Cruise missile is a small and mobile weapon, any verification of locations and numbers is extremely difficult. It is also difficult to detect whether the missile is armed with a conventional or nuclear warhead. Capable of being fired from many different kinds of launchers, such missiles lack the visible anchor of ballistic missiles — the silos or submarines specially fitted to fire ballistic missiles. Such verification is vital because neither superpower will enter into an agreement to limit nuclear weapons if there is no reliable means of monitoring compliance.

In general, a verification system consists of a complex of people, hardware, treaty clauses and procedures which is supposed to fulfil two basic purposes in connection with arms control or disarmament treaties. The first is to deter the parties to a treaty from violating it in any particular way by making the risk of being caught greater than the value of that particular violation, including very small ones. The second is to make certain that a major violation — or a conjunction of a large number of small violations — of the kind that could create a really significant change in the military balance is detected in time for the necessary counteraction to be taken.

At least until the development of the modern strategic Cruise missile, successful disarmament agreements with the USSR have not had to rely on the honesty of the Soviets. As former CIA directors Herbert Scoville and William Colby and many other experts have acknowledged, American intelligence could effectively monitor the Russians under comprehensive agreements. The arms limitation or disarmament treaties could be monitored by satellites, radar and other means possessed by both sides and used to police the various arms agreements that have been adopted in the past. For example, U.S. satellites continually cross over Soviet territory and provide highly detailed photographs of features on the ground below. Other satellites carry sensitive infra-red detectors which can follow the hot exhaust of missiles and aircraft in flight and can even penetrate darkness to produce detailed pictures of Soviet activities on the surface or even underground. Satellite-based radar systems penetrate cloud cover and fog as well as darkness. Complex cameras known as multispectral scanners have the capacity to reveal even camouflaged objects. In addition to its satellites, the U.S. has radar and radio receiving equipment located on the ground, on aircraft, on ships and even in submarines. Information is recorded, analyzed and, if necessary, decoded by teams of experts. The most advanced and powerful computer systems assist in each of these tasks.

The United States reportedly has the capacity to follow certain Soviet weapon systems from their initial appearance in a design bureau (where preliminary designs are drafted and prototypes are constructed) through to their testing, production and deployment. Former U.S. Secretary of Defense Harold Brown has said: "Our national technical means enable us to monitor all key aspects of Soviet strategic programs, including the development, testing, production, deployment, training and operation of Soviet strategic capabilities. We can perform these tasks despite the closed nature of Soviet society." And the U.S. Defense Department, the State Department and the Joint Chiefs of Staff have stated that "Soviet compliance performance under fourteen arms control agreements has been good." If one asks whether it is theoretically possible that one side could cheat on some individual phase of weapons development without the certainty of being detected, the answer is maybe; as to whether it could cheat enough to gain significantly, the answer is no.

Indeed, American verification capabilities are growing rapidly. The $300-million satellite put in orbit by the secret U.S. space shuttle flight in January of 1984 has two to three times the gathering ability of other satellites and can be used for tracking Soviet missiles and eavesdropping on Soviet military and diplomatic communications. The satellite can also monitor Soviet radio broadcasts and signals. In 1986, the U.S. plans to launch a spy satellite called KH-12, which will be able to distinguish objects four to six inches across and provide sharp pictures of any part of the globe, even at night.

Still, these formidable technical capabilities may have met their match in the Cruise. The problems of each type of deployment — by ground, air and sea — will be examined in turn.

Some critics charge that ground-launched Cruise missiles can be hidden in trucks, moving vans, railway cars, garages, small boats or almost anywhere under tarpaulin and when so hidden cannot be detected by surveillance satellites. This school of thought holds that Cruise missiles can be hidden in back-yard garages and launched at a moment's notice. But as Jack Ruina of the Massachusetts Institute of Technology points out: "Sure [the Cruise] is small, but no one is going to have Cruise missiles running around like they have milk trucks or oil trucks. There's a whole command and control structure. It's going to be on a military base." While each GLCM is less than twenty feet long, the TEL vehicle (its "transporter-erector-launcher") which carries four missiles is itself about fifty feet in length. Furthermore, each GLCM combat unit consists of sixteen missiles loaded on four TELs accompanied by two mobile launch control centre vans (LCCs) which provide communications and computer support. GLCM convoys will hardly be unobtrusive. The difficulty of distinguishing a nuclear GLCM from a conventional Cruise missile remains troublesome.

70 Misguided Missiles

However, given the relatively small number of GLCMs being produced and deployed, they are not presently as much of a problem as the two remaining launching systems.

SALT II established a procedure whereby the numbers of air-launched Cruise missiles are to be controlled through limits both on the number of bombers allowed to be fitted with Cruise missile launchers and on the number of Cruise missiles to be carried by each bomber. The SALT II process established the precedent of "worst case" counting rules for ALCMs on bombers, although the scheme could be used for missiles on any type of aircraft. As mandated by the SALT II agreement, the unique wing characteristics of these bombers ("functionally-related observable differences," or FRODs) allow Soviet satellites to identify them as Cruise missile carriers. Using the SALT rules, a maximum allowed missile load for each type of aircraft would be established in negotiations. Every aircraft of a certain type would be considered to have a certain missile load, regardless of what it actually carried, thereby eliminating the need to count individual missiles. Any aircraft detected with a configuration suggesting it could accommodate more than the maximum allowed number would be grounds for suspicion that cheating was being attempted. All Soviet ALCMs are currently externally mounted, making the detection of altered missile loads relatively easy. The task would become more difficult were the Soviets to develop internal mountings, although a development of this sort would probably be detected as the aircraft was modified.

In addition to negotiating limits on nuclear-armed ALCMs, conventional ALCMs would have to be distinguishable from their nuclear counterparts. This could only be achieved by agreeing to limit nuclear ALCMs to bombers identified by FRODs — as is done now — and by developing distinctive conventional ALCMs that cannot be easily modified into nuclear missiles. Can satisfactory design features be developed for discriminating between Cruise missiles with tactical ranges and conventional warheads and those with longer ranges and nuclear explosives? The design features could be of two types: FRODs which physically limit the capabilities of a weapon system so it cannot be confused with another — for example, dimensional limits that preclude fuel loads for longer ranges; and "externally observable design features" (EODFs) which would signal one side's intentions to the other but not actually limit a weapon's capabilities. An example of an EODF would be the elimination of B-52s or B-1s as short-range or tactical Cruise missile carriers. Alternatively, changing the length of the short-range Cruise missile by two or three feet to make it observably different from the ALCMs could be considered. While by no means easy, establishing confidence in ALCM verification should be possible, accepting that the degree of confidence will not be as high as in the monitoring of other nuclear delivery vehicles.

Of all the variants of Cruise missiles, experts generally agree that none has complicated arms control efforts as much as the SLCM. SLCMs pose all the verification problems common to Cruise missiles, and then some. First, plans are to put strategic long-range SLCMs aboard traditionally non-strategic vessels (major surface combatants and attack submarines). Second, nuclear SLCMs will be placed alongside non-nuclear SLCMs from which they are indistinguishable (of the 4,000 Cruise missiles scheduled to be deployed on U.S. battleships, destroyers, cruisers and submarines, fewer than 1,000 will carry nuclear warheads). Third, ships and submarines can hold a large number of SLCMs. A single destroyer can hold upwards of 120 in vertical launches. Fourth, stored in torpedo rooms of submarines and launched from torpedo tubes, SLCMs will be impossible to detect and count even with verification procedures far more impressive than those that exist today.

One possible solution to this quandary is to ban all land-attack SLCMs. This could be accomplished by prohibiting SLCMs with ranges in excess of the longest anti-ship version (250 to 500 miles). Theoretically, range limits on new Cruise missiles are verifiable, even though Cruise missile range is difficult to define and estimate precisely. Flight-test telemetry can be monitored and along with other observed missile characteristics can be used to determine range on the basis of the fuel consumption rate and estimated fuel capacity. Such a ban would be extremely difficult to negotiate today because Cruise range is quite different at various altitudes and speeds, and because both the U.S. and the USSR have already tested long-range ALCMs and their development programs are far along.

If it is not possible to ban land-attack SLCMs, their deployment might be constrained in other ways to reduce counting problems. SLCMs could be prohibited from deployment aboard attack submarines, which are probably the most difficult platform from which to count them. Devices to detect gamma-ray emanations from nuclear weapons could periodically be placed aboard submarines and ships not permitted to carry nuclear SLCMs. Even if this measure could not be negotiated, a maximum allowable loading could be established for ships and their SLCMs (no more than x number of launchers on x number of ships and submarines). Unlike aircraft, however, ships store all their Cruise missiles internally where they cannot be counted. It would be difficult to determine, therefore, if any individual ship were reaching the loading limit. This uncertainty could be decreased by restrictions on SLCM launchers, which would be much easier to count than the missiles themselves. The launcher is an integral part of the ship and for the most part is distinguishable from afar. The U.S. and Soviet Union could agree on which type of launchers to use for nuclear-capable missiles and set a limit on the number of such launchers that could be deployed on any single ship of a certain class. Certain types of launchers for SLCMs (armoured box and vertical launch systems, for example) are easier to count.

Submarine-launched SLCMs are not as amenable to such launcher counting because the newer type of Cruise missile is launched from submarine torpedo tubes. Even if it were not possible to reach an agreement by (1) permitting long-range Cruise missiles on only those types of ships and submarines that have external launchers with no re-load mechanisms, (2) forbidding testing and deployment of SLCMs from submarine torpedo tubes, (3) providing for SLCM loading to take place in the open and (4) designating factories where SLCMs are built so production can be determined more accurately, a maximum allowable loading for submarine-launched SLCMs could still be established. The prospective cheater might still beat this limit, but a submarine is not the roomiest of vessels and any attempt to increase the missile loading significantly would probably cause a severe degradation of the submarine's operational capabilities.

These SLCM verification measures, whether used singly or collectively, cannot promise full monitoring confidence. Indeed, at the lower end of the scale we arrive at the borderline where verification potential threatens to become insufficient. Christopher Paine of the Federation of American Scientists has said: "The nuclear SLCM represents a monstrous and wholly gratuitous complication for arms control — which is perhaps why the Reagan administration is so enthusiastic about it."

But while many characteristics of the Cruise missile and its deployment present challenges to existing means of verification, Cruise missiles need not represent a hopeless task for arms control. Methods can be found to facilitate the monitoring of American and Soviet Cruise missiles. Cruise missile verification problems are by no means trivial, but they are not insurmountable. According to Robert Scott, editor of *Arms Control Today*, a publication of the non-partisan Washington-based Arms Control Association, with technological ingenuity "You can always find ways to verify these things — and with Cruise missiles there is still time."

In summary, verification measures could combine range limits in the form of size restrictions, limits on deployment areas and the rate and amount of permissible redeployment, functionally related or externally observable differences, and counting rules that assume the "worst case." Though Cruise missiles are easier to conceal than ballistic missiles, they are no more so than other weapon systems (anti-aircraft missiles, tanks, etc.) that both superpowers presently count with a great deal of precision. It would be extremely difficult and politically risky for the Soviets or the Americans to conceal large-scale deployment of Cruise missiles.

Ultimately, the greatest challenge to arms control may be the American attitude toward it. In contrast to previous administrations which have acknowledged that the Soviets have respected arms control treaties, President Reagan has claimed that the Soviets have been violating an array of arms control agreements, including SALT II. The Federation of American Scientists, after reviewing the evidence, contends that some of the Reagan administration's charges are based on "ambiguous" or "meager" evidence and that other charges describe not violations but the Soviets taking advantage of loose language in the treaties. Furthermore, the federation states, "none of the activities in question constitutes a tangible military threat."

Washington's charges are also inconsistent. For example, the Reagan administration claims that the throw weight, or payload capacity, of the SS-25 missile is greater than that of its predecessor, the SS-13, by more than the five per cent that is permitted by the provisions of SALT II. The Americans also charge the Soviets with interfering illegally with the ability of the U.S. to collect data from Russian flight tests. While the Soviets may, in fact, be stretching the rules, any claim that Moscow has impeded (the technical term is "encrypted") flight-test verification would appear to be undercut by the detailed charges the U.S. has levelled concerning the SS-13 and SS-25 throw-weight comparison, since precise data is certainly required to make such a judgment.

There may very well be a hidden motivation for the Reagan administration's accusations. To undermine the foundations of existing arms treaties with charges of violations would fit in neatly with Washington's plans to move forward with an arms build-up. Spurgeon Keeny, deputy director of the Arms Control and Disarmament Agency during Jimmy Carter's administration, has noted that "there are forces within the Reagan administration who would like to use questions of compliance as a device to undercut confidence in the whole treaty regime."

When viewed in isolation, the deployment of Cruise missiles does pose significant monitoring difficulties, but these problems would certainly be eased by a comprehensive agreement such as the nuclear freeze. A comprehensive nuclear freeze would place a *series* of hurdles in the way of a prospective cheater. To be successful, the cheater would have to produce the plutonium or uranium secretly, and clandestinely fashion it into a warhead. Any warhead testing would also have to be illicit. Furthermore, inherent in a comprehensive freeze would be an "intra-agreement" deterrent to cheating on the elements less easy to monitor. The prospective cheater would have to consider that to be caught in or even suspected of one violation could jeopardize the other elements of the agreement. For example, the Soviet Union could be deterred from cheating on Cruise missile deployment because of the fear that it might result in the United States unilaterally renouncing parts of the treaty the Soviets greatly value. Unfortunately a nuclear freeze is totally at odds with current American nuclear weapons strategy, the subject of the following chapter.

3
Nuclear War-Fighting

Washington is pressing ahead with its $2.6-trillion military build-up, which will add approximately 17,000 strategic nuclear weapons to the U.S. arsenal over the period 1982-1989. The United States seeks nuclear weapons superiority — not simply parity, much less a mere deterrent. Richard Perle, assistant secretary of defense, has joked that he and like-minded officials were going to "teach the nation a lesson in supply side arms control." He obviously meant there would be years of unilateral build-up in American "defenses." Richard Burt, just before he assumed a senior position in the State Department in 1981, advocated just such a revamped strategy of nuclear escalation: "A new emphasis," he said, "must be placed on generating nuclear responses that are militarily meaningful." He went on to call for "a broader concept for nuclear use" and for "American forces [that] are capable of waging a large scale, sustained nuclear campaign." Such thinking has become quite commonplace in Washington.

Paul Warnke, former U.S. chief arms control negotiator, is among those who have witnessed a hawkish shift in U.S. foreign policy from the inside and now warn of aggressive use of American nuclear weapons:

> There are disturbing signs of a growing reliance on nuclear weapons as an instrument of foreign policy — to gain political ends, not just to prevent nuclear

attack. Some advisors to the current administration have stated categorically that we should "devise ways to employ nuclear war rationally." Other Administration officials have maintained that the goal of our nuclear arsenal should be to prevent others from using conventional military force against our interests while leaving us free to utilize our own conventional force as we see fit. And the argument that nuclear arms are useful only for deterrence seems now to be losing ground to the argument that we can and should shape our forces to fight and survive and win a nuclear war.

War-fighting strategies require highly accurate weapons that can hit military and industrial targets. The Cruise missile is just such a weapon. As Ernie Regehr, research director of Project Ploughshares, argues, "The Cruise missile is dedicated to the proposition that it is possible to fight and 'prevail' in a nuclear war. It seeks to present nuclear war as a viable alternative and it is this that makes it an immensely dangerous weapon."

The First-Use Tradition

The deployment of nuclear weapons for purposes other than deterrence is not a new practice. American nuclear strategy has never been based on a doctrine of pure deterrence. A strategic balance which would merely suffice to deter nuclear attacks on American and Soviet home territories "has always been rejected as a totally inadequate standard for nuclear negotiations," according to Eugene Rostow, former director of the U.S. Arms Control and Disarmament Agency. The version of deterrence pursued by the United States over the years has been remarkably elastic, all-encompassing and ambitious; the goal, in the words of the Centre for Defense Information, has been to deter "any Soviet actions that we do not like." The name analysts give this doctrine is "extended deterrence."

The possible first use of nuclear weapons has been an underlying premise of U.S. foreign policy since 1950, when Paul Nitze (now a chief arms negotiator for President Reagan) wrote a top-secret, presidentially approved National Security Council memorandum:

> Our overall policy [on nuclear weapons] at the present time may be described as one designed to foster a world environment in which the American system can survive and flourish.... Without superior aggregate military strength being readily mobilizable, a policy of containment — which is in effect a policy of calculated and gradual coercion — is no more than a policy of bluff.

The American strategy has been to establish conventional military power of a strength and mobility designed expressly to overwhelm the revolutionary movements or military forces of most Third World nations, while counting on unquestionable superiority in nuclear weapons to hold the Soviet Union at bay should it wish it to contest any invasion or intervention resulting from this strategy. The nuclear threat could also be used against weaker adversaries. The 1950s and early 1960s were dubbed by U.S. Secretary of Defense John Foster Dulles as the era of "massive retaliation." American nuclear strategy was loudly broadcast as entailing "instant" and massive response to Soviet aggression.

On numerous occasions, senior U.S. officials did consider using the atomic bomb. According to a Brookings Institution study prepared in cooperation with the Department of Defense, Washington threatened the use of nuclear weapons no less than eighteen times between 1946 and 1970. Daniel Ellsberg, a former military analyst for the Pentagon, has noted that "every President from Truman on (with the exception of Ford) has had occasion in an ongoing crisis to direct serious preparation for possible U.S. initiation of tactical nuclear warfare. Preparation in every case 'leaked' to the enemy, in several cases accompanied by secret, explicit, official threats."

The Soviet Union has also used the threat of nuclear weapons in conflicts with weaker nations. Moscow showed bomb test films to President Tito of Yugoslavia and to the Shah of Iran on the eve of important negotiations with them. In the 1956 Suez crisis, the Soviets threatened France and England with Soviet missiles. During the border conflict with China, the Soviets made verbal threats concerning the use of nuclear weapons. And Soviet troops carried tactical nuclear weapons in their 1968 invasion of Czechoslovakia. These instances of Soviet "nuclear signalling" are not dissimilar (except with respect to the number of threats made) to American attempts to use the threat of nuclear involvement. As is most often the case in the nuclear arms race, there is more than enough blame to go around.

There have been, of course, many conflicts in which U.S. intervention has not involved the nuclear threat. In these cases, nuclear coercion was either unnecessary or simply not worth expending on the limited objectives involved. For instance, it would have been both wasteful and unrealistic to use or threaten to use atomic arms in the CIA-sponsored overthrow of the Guatemalan government in 1954, when planes and artillery pieces were more than adequate. Ellsberg concludes:

> Our military strategy has been based, ever since the debut of atomic weapons in 1945, on our possible first use of nuclear weapons. Again and again, generally in secret from the American public, U.S. nuclear weapons have been used, in the precise way that a gun is used when you point it at someone's head in a direct confrontation, whether or not the trigger is pulled.

Thus nuclear weapons need never be detonated to do their destructive work. As instruments of political and economic intimidation, they serve to maintain an international order in which extraordinary benefits flow to the powerful and extraordinary costs accrue to the powerless. American foreign and military policy has been based on the premise that to protect vital U.S. interests around the world, Washington has to be able to persuade all adversaries, real or imagined, that the United States would not shrink from using nuclear weapons to achieve its ends. That was the message that the Kennedy administration sent to Nikita Khrushchev in the Cuban missile crisis. It was Richard Nixon's proposed "madman" solution to the Vietnam war. It is, today, the reason why the Reagan administration refuses to forswear the first use of nuclear arms.

Yet the translation of U.S. strategic superiority into effective "on the ground" supremacy has proven to be a will-o'-the-wisp, especially in Third World conflicts in which the Soviet Union was not directly involved. There is considerable doubt whether many of the American nuclear threats were the decisive factor in containing the Soviet Union and intimidating Third World nations. American public opinion seriously constrained the options for U.S. officials and consequently made their nuclear threats less credible.

However, what policy-makers believe to be true is often more important than what is true.

Almost all of these threats were made in the context of an overwhelming U.S. strategic superiority. By the mid-1970s, when the U.S. lost its clear nuclear margin, the ability to make such nuclear threats effectively had eroded seriously. Henry Kissinger thought that this change constituted a "strategic revolution," meaning that the U.S. could no longer restrain the Russians from regional intervention.

Among American war planners, nuclear parity was viewed as giving licence to Soviet expansionism. Their fears were reinforced when Cuban troops were dispatched to Angola and Ethiopia, and when Soviet forces marched into Afghanistan. Between 1974 and 1980 some fourteen revolutions took place in Asia, Africa and Latin America. Though due largely to indigenous pressures, these upheavals were seen in the United States as the product of Russian meddling and Western weakness. Added to these responses was the attitude that as American economic dominance of the world faltered, economic survival was more than ever dependent on access to overseas markets and raw materials. As well, American strategists campaigned to reverse the "Vietnam syndrome" and to rehabilitate intervention as a means of dealing with turbulence in the Third World, particularly in the Middle East. Along with the sense of declining U.S. nuclear — and conventional — superiority, these factors inspired a shift under President Carter (1976-80) toward a more overt enunciation of first-use doctrine.

Not surprisingly, it was the most prized overseas resource of all — Mid-East oil — that brought the first-use doctrine out in the open. Upheaval in Iran, a key client state of the U.S., posed the theoretical threat of Soviet invasion in 1979. The press reported that after the Shah was overthrown, President Carter had dispatched a naval flotilla, including tactical nuclear weapons, to the Persian Gulf. Shortly thereafter, the president announced the "Carter Doctrine," which stated that "any attempt by an outside force to gain control of the Persian Gulf region would be regarded as an assault on the vital interests of the United States" and would be "repelled by the use of any means necessary."

Since the Pentagon had acknowledged that U.S. conventional forces were incapable of turning back a Soviet invasion, "any means" could only refer to nuclear arms. The message to the USSR was that the U.S. was prepared to respond to conventional attacks with nuclear weapons. The threat was made explicit shortly after the speech introducing the doctrine, in a story in the *New York Times* — thought to be a leak from the administration — about a 1979 Defense Department study. According to the *Times*, the study said that "to prevail in an Iranian scenario, we might have to threaten or make use of tactical nuclear weapons."

Soon after the Iranian crisis, U.S. policy took another sharp turn, this time toward a "nuclear war winning capability," with the Carter administration's Presidential Directive 59. This document called for developing a capacity to wage "prolonged but limited nuclear war" until an outcome "favourable" to the U.S. was reached. It emphasized the need to be able to make precise and limited attacks against the USSR, a function to which the Cruise missile is ideally suited. The directive's targeting list (a menu of 40,000 installations, according to one report) included the following Soviet assets:

- 700 leadership targets involving underground shelters and therefore constituting "hard" targets (those demanding precise accuracy);
- 2,000 strategic force targets including 1,400 ICBM silos plus command-control bunkers, nuclear strategic sites and strategic air and naval facilities, most of which are also hard targets;
- 3,000 "other" military targets including 500 air fields, military units, supply depots and key transportation hubs, most of which are soft targets and many of which are large area targets;
- 200 to 400 "key factories" which would presumably be war mobilization and production facilities and would be relatively soft targets.

That the Carter Doctrine signalled that the U.S. was turning its back on deterrence was made clear by Carter's national security adviser, Zbigniew Brzezinski, who justified the directive this way:

> I assumed that our pre-existing doctrine of threatened mutual destruction only made sense while we were in a superior position over the Soviets. We could scare them with this doctrine because in practice it meant: We will destroy you, but you cannot destroy us. As the situation grew more equal, this doctrine became less convincing.

When asked if the Carter policy of "flexible response" included limited nuclear war, Brzezinski replied: "If necessary that includes limited nuclear war ... but when one side is capable of carrying it out and the other isn't, then the side that has that capability is in a better position to negotiate in a crisis situation."

In other words, what the U.S. is seeking in its quest for war-fighting capacity and plans for the selective use of weapons is a functional equivalent of the overwhelming nuclear superiority of the past — it is seeking to restore political utility to its strategic forces.

Needless to say, the Reagan administration, which took office in 1980, was not inclined to reverse the direction of the Carter Doctrine. Deputy Secretary of Defense Frank Carlucci said in January of 1981: "I think we need to have a counterforce capability [weapons capable of attacking Soviet weapons]. Over and above that, I think we need to have a [nuclear] warfighting capability." Later in the year, Defense Secretary Caspar Weinberger declared: "We set out to achieve improved capabilities to enhance deterrence and U.S. capabilities to prevail should deterrence fail."

The Quest for Nuclear Superiority

For strategists and officials like Weinberger, the credibility of U.S. extended deterrence depends not just on simple American nuclear superiority, but on superiority at all points along the spectrum of violence. It is felt that the USSR would be much less likely to aid its Third World allies if the U.S. held nuclear superiority. Or if the U.S. intervened in the Middle East or Third World, Moscow would be less likely to develop a counter response, for fear of making the next move in a scenario in which the U.S. held the winning hand. But the U.S. would have to be able to demonstrate its superiority at every possible step in a "ladder of escalation." It would control the level of exchange by effectively deterring the other side from escalating. According to this theory of "escalation dominance," political and military leaders should enjoy the flexibility of selecting from a "menu of options," both nuclear and conventional. In particular, the U.S. should never be in a position where it would be deterred from using nuclear weapons first. Otherwise, the American nuclear arsenal would be rendered useless by what Reagan advisor Colin Gray has called "the paralyzing impact of self deterrence." The belief in the need for escalation dominance is echoed by Richard Perle, Reagan's assistant secretary of defense:

> I've been worried less about what would happen in an actual nuclear exchange than about the effect that the nuclear balance has on our willingness to take risks in local situations. It is not that I am worried about the Soviets attacking the United States with nuclear weapons confident that they will win that nuclear war. It is that I worry about an American President's feeling he cannot afford to take action in a crisis because Soviet nuclear forces are such that, if escalation took place, they are better poised than we are to move up the escalation ladder.

Such prognostications always presuppose a benign role for the United States: America is assumed to be the defender, the other side the aggressor. Hence, supporters of the nuclear option claim it is necessary to the defense of free societies against aggression, whereas if such a posture were adopted by the Soviet Union it would be said to constitute an unacceptable risk to peace. The "margin of superiority" in nuclear weapons is justified as imposing constraints on the USSR while removing the constraints on U.S. behaviour. As General John W. Vessey, chairman of the Joint Chiefs of Staff, summarized the issue: "We don't want a war and we certainly don't want a nuclear war. But at the same time we don't want to be paralyzed by the fear of war as we pursue our economic, political, social and cultural objectives." Explaining that strategic superiority is the key factor enabling the U.S. to restore order to an increasingly turbulent Third World, Eugene Rostow has argued that "the nuclear weapon is a pervasive influence in all aspects of diplomacy and of conventional war, and in a crisis we could go forward in planning the use of our conventional forces with great freedom because we knew the Soviet Union could not escalate beyond the local level."

As some of these statements suggest, the U.S. readily mixes conventional and nuclear forces on its strategic chessboard. At government hearings in 1984, General Ellis, speaking for the Strategic Air Command, expressed the belief that it is no longer possible to draw a line between nuclear and conventional weapons. He was devising possible American responses to Soviet activity in South Asia and Africa. Such contingency planning involved limited and regional nuclear options and called for combat missions by heavy bombers which could be flown west over the Pacific and Indian Oceans to the Middle East. There is no way to interpret such military strategy other than as a warning to the Soviet Union that, as in the specific case of Iran, America now has general plans to make a limited nuclear strike in response to a conventional attack on an area it considers vital.

In fact the U.S. might decide to respond to such an attack on another front altogether. Shortly after taking office, Reagan administration strategists reportedly issued guidelines to the military "to hit the Soviets at their remote and vulnerable outposts in retaliation for any cutoff of Persian Gulf oil." In the view of Secretary of Defense Caspar Weinberger, "Our deterrent capability in the Persian Gulf is linked with our ability and willingness to shift or widen the war to other areas." In effect, Weinberger was saying that the strategy of extended deterrence would assume larger proportions; if Soviet forces were to invade the Persian Gulf region, the United States should have the capability to hit back there or in Cuba, Libya, Vietnam, or the Asian land mass of the Soviet Union itself.

The increasing technological sophistication of many Third World armies also encourages an American nuclear response. Since U.S. conventional forces could well be overwhelmed, nuclear weapons have been integrated with intervention policy, making the unimaginable far more possible.

Planning for Limited Nuclear War

How can the United States ensure that its use of tactical nuclear weapons, or its threatened use, would not lead to a two-way exchange, the prospect of which would deter use in the first place? Edward Luttwak, an advisor to President Reagan, makes the rather bold assumption that if the United States launches a limited attack in a real conflict Moscow will "know what the U.S. is up to and will show restraint."

If some retaliation does occur, how can Washington keep it limited — to an "acceptable" level? The Pentagon's answer is that the U.S. must have a threat of escalating the conflict that is more "credible" than the Soviets can make, should they choose to match Washington in a local area with nuclear retaliation. This means being able not only to escalate, say to a region wide level, but to escalate again and again, if necessary, to a level where the Soviets will be unable or afraid to match American weapons. That calls for forces superior to those of the Soviets at virtually every level of nuclear conflict, up to a fully-disarming first strike or a campaign of annihilation.

Nuclear War-Fighting 89

The accuracy of a new generation of nuclear missiles inspires faith that their use will not necessarily result in mutual destruction. Planners suggest that it is possible to fire nuclear warning shots, to fight and win a nuclear war, to employ "clean" nuclear weapons, and so on. Colin Gray, one of the most articulate and forceful members of the school of strategic thought currently dominant in Washington, advocates the MX missile for precisely these reasons:

> The United States has a fundamental foreign policy requirement that its strategic nuclear forces provide credible limited first strike options.... Overall MX should be thought of as a weapon system that is essential for the support of forward placed allies, in that supported limited first strike options could be threatened credibly, secure in the knowledge that the United States had a residual ICBM force that could deter attack upon itself.

It is a deeply held view of many U.S. strategists that a margin of nuclear superiority enables the U.S. to win in Third World crises. This view is scarcely susceptible to empirical verification but its proponents — who occupy the highest national security positions in the U.S. government — clearly believe it to be the case. And fueling the drive for nuclear modernization is the American belief that the U.S. could not manage the Third World upheavals of the 1970s because it had lost that margin. Richard Burt, now director of the State Department's Bureau of Political Military Affairs and formerly responsible for *New York Times* coverage of such national security issues, believes that "the nuclear balance is the crucial barometer of Soviet willingness to take risks and nurture crisis in trouble spots around the world." Yet the power of extended deterrence is hardly unlimited. It is unrealistic to assume, for example, that Soviet support for Nicaragua would diminish once the Pershing II were deployed, or that the Iranians would not have taken U.S. diplomats hostage had the MX been deployed. However, as long as Washington believes in the effectiveness of nuclear threats, the drive for useable nuclear superiority will continue. In January of 1980, Carter's secretary of defense, Harold Brown, explained that administration's build-up:

> The programmed rates of growth are needed for two reasons ... sustained expansion of the Soviet defense effort ... [and] the growth in international turbulence, illustrated by recent developments in the Caribbean, South East Asia, Korea, Afghanistan and Iran.... Our strategic [nuclear] capabilities provide the foundation on which our security rests ... with them, our other forces become meaningful instruments of military and political power....

Increasingly, the purpose of the ongoing nuclear arms race is, from the point of view of the United States, to give the U.S. greater freedom to intervene in developing countries without risking a conventional challenge on the part of the Soviet Union. The threat to use nuclear weapons is not, of course, so much a basis to resort deliberately to nuclear war as it is to participate and persevere in an escalatory process, even though it might result in nuclear war. Eugene Rostow has defined deterrence in so many words: "to confront Soviet expansion through the use of aggression with the prospect of unacceptable risk, to which they have always responded with prudence."

The rather predictable irony of the rationale behind limited war is that the U.S. expects to limit the scope of war by adding to its arsenal. The goal, according to a critical passage of the 1982 U.S. Defense Guidance statement, is for American nuclear forces to "prevail and be able to force the Soviet Union to seek earliest possible termination of hostilities on terms favorable to the United States."

On this note, it is interesting to look at the original definition of escalation dominance, set out twenty years ago by Herman Kahn:

> this is a capacity, other things being equal, to enable the side possessing it to enjoy marked advantages in a given region of the escalation ladder…. It depends on the net effect of the competing capabilities on the rung being occupied, the estimate by each side of what would happen if the confrontation moved to these other rungs, and the means each side has to shift the confrontation to these other rungs.

Can the possibility of limiting or controlling a nuclear war — so neatly set out in theory — really be accepted as a rational basis for military planning? The thought that the contending parties would abide by some undefined Marquess of Queensbury rules and proceed in gentlemanly fashion to lob warheads at one another without major escalation is far from the reality in the fog of war. Assessing damage, determining the opponent's intentions, deciding on a proper response, communicating that decision reliably and maintaining control over military forces so that the actual response matches the original decision are all notoriously difficult to achieve even in conventional war.

Nuclear war would not resemble a kind of ping-pong game in which nuclear warheads would drop precisely and discriminately on military installations — the proximity of many Soviet military targets to urban centres makes it impossible to keep collateral damage from going beyond "acceptable" levels. Even after the current ambitious upgrade of the U.S. command and control system is completed, its designers believe that at best it could withstand an attack involving a few hundred nuclear warheads before losing positive control over the U.S. arsenal. This pattern will of course also be true on the other side. As Reagan advisor General Brent Scowcroft remarked: "There's a real dilemma here that we haven't sorted out. The kinds of controlled nuclear options to which we're moving presume communication with the Soviet Union; and yet, from a military point of view, one of the most efficient kinds of attack is against leadership and command and control systems."

The unlikelihood of limiting an exchange was hinted at by Henry Kissinger in 1965, when he wrote: "No one knows how governments or people will react to a nuclear explosion under conditions where both sides possess vast arsenals." This was understood by former U.S. Defense Secretary Robert McNamara and three other retired American State Department officials:

> It is time to recognize that no one has ever succeeded in advancing any persuasive reason to believe that any use of nuclear weapons, even on the smallest scale, could reliably be expected to remain limited. Every serious analysis and every military exercise, for over 25 years, has demonstrated that even the most restrained battlefield use would be enormously destructive to civilian life and property. There is no way for anyone to have any confidence that such a nuclear action will not lead to further and more devastating exchanges.

A similar judgment was given by Desmond Ball for the International Institute for Strategic Studies in its major study on the likelihood of controlling nuclear war:

> Nuclear weapons are simply too powerful and have too many disparate effects, not all of which are predictable, and some of which may currently not even be appreciated. Any nuclear attacks of military or strategic significance, beyond those intended merely to demonstrate political resolve, are likely to produce millions of casualties.... Moreover, the dynamics of a nuclear exchange are likely to generate military and political pressures for the relaxation of restraints, even where both adversaries agreed at the outset that it was in their mutual interest to avoid unwanted escalation.

As arms control expert Paul Bracken has pointed out, the relaxation of restraints would in fact probably begin sometime earlier: leaders adhering to a limited nuclear war policy "might end up bumbling into a nuclear war with a vague belief in its controllability."

Should the U.S. be on the receiving end of the first blow, it would do well to follow the advice of McGeorge Bundy, National Security Advisor to Presidents Kennedy and Johnson, that the American retaliatory strike be at a lesser level. Bundy's hope was that such an exchange could be controlled, but any resemblance between a lesser-response strategy and nuclear war-fighting planning is coincidental. The latter is based on the deployment of the widest possible array of nuclear weapons needed to "win" a nuclear war, while the former is dependent on only a survivable second-strike deterrent force.

The Role of the Cruise

As we saw in Chapter 2, the Cruise missile is essentially designed as a weapon to fight in a so-called limited nuclear war — as a "surgical" weapon for precise strategic targets. With great accuracy, low cost, evasive ability and the possibility of early deployment in large numbers, it fits well into schemes of escalation dominance. In the official Pentagon document, "U.S. Military Posture F.Y. [Fiscal Year] 1984," the Joint Chiefs of Staff state that "if deterrence fails, nuclear weapons such as the cruise and Pershing II would make it possible to escalate the intensity of the conflict in a controlled manner."

Albert Wohlstetter, an influential defense advisor to President Reagan, has noted that attacking military targets on land

> effectively with the huge inaccuracies expected in the late 1950s would have meant filling an enormous area of uncertainty with destruction. That might typically have subjected an area of 1,000 square miles or so to unintended lethal effects. By contrast, a current Cruise missile, with midcourse guidance and a small nuclear warhead, could be equally effective against a military target while confining lethal damage to less than one square mile.

According to former Defense Secretary Harold Brown, the Cruise missile "would probably be the best weapon against hardened targets, except time-urgent targets because it would take eight hours to get there, but at [censored] feet accuracy it has the highest kill probability against hard targets of any of our forces."

One such category of hard targets is Soviet missile silos. If the Russians were successful in creating "cold-launch" missiles — which do not need hot booster rockets to get started and hence do not destroy their silos — they would be able to use their silos repeatedly, responding to an initial American attack with a series of retaliatory strikes. But the Cruise missile, no matter how slow, could be used to penetrate Soviet defenses and destroy the silos before they could be reloaded, thus freeing the far faster and more versatile intercontinental missiles for other offensive tasks.

The primary mission of the sea-launched Cruise missiles, according to U.S. Navy Secretary John Lehman, is to attack Soviet supply depots, railroads, transport centres and similar targets in "mopping-up operations" after a full scale nuclear attack with ballistic missiles. Adm. Frank B. Kelso, director of the Navy's Strategic Submarine Division, has testified that SLCMs would help the United States "retain a measure of coercive power in the post-exchange environment." Thus, as Ambassador Gerard Smith, chief negotiator for the SALT I Treaty under Nixon, pointed out, the deployment of sea-launched missiles will "give credence to the growing apprehension that the U.S. is not only preparing to fight a nuclear war, but that it is also planning to fight a protracted nuclear war, if such can be imagined."

In terms of projecting power on other fronts, the Cruise could be deployed against targets in the Middle East, Asia or Africa. The Cruise missiles in Sicily are easily aimed at the Middle East and North Africa, and Asia is threatened by Cruise missiles in the seas of Japan. All these locations are flash points where a conventional American military activity could suddenly escalate to include the use of "small" and accurate nuclear weapons designed to put a quick end to a conventional war. It is now unlikely that the U.S. Navy could generate TERCOM maps for each of a large number of possible Third World targets, but that difficulty would be eliminated by the satellite-based global positioning guidance systems under development.

During the last month of the Carter administration, the chief of naval operations ordered "the revitalization of the Navy's tactical nuclear capabilities." The Reagan administration has funded this development. An important element in Reagan's "1983 Defense Authorization Act" concerns the procurement of new supercarriers, core units of new, exceptionally potent nuclear-capable naval squadrons. These are designed to strike directly at the heart of Soviet defenses. Speaking at a congressional hearing in March of 1984, Adm. James D. Watkins, chief of naval operations, translated this new posture into layman's terms: "We go for the jugular." The Congressional Budget Office (CBO) explains: "The specifics of these plans are based upon a maritime offensive strategy that emphasizes strikes against enemy forces and their supporting base structure, including strikes in enemy waters against its home territory." In the words of Navy Secretary Lehman, these operations are intended to keep "the Soviets concerned with threats all around the periphery." As ships and submarines begin to carry long-range Cruise missiles, they will represent not only tactical assets that the Russians will seek to neutralize but also regional and strategic nuclear forces to be destroyed at all costs. The CBO report notes: "Critics of this position view the strategy as fundamentally unworkable and likely to provoke Soviet use of nuclear weapons against the [carrier] battle groups." The strategy is considered "dangerously provocative in a nuclear-armed world and very hazardous to U.S. carrier forces even if a nuclear exchange is avoided."

For theatre warfare, there is the nuclear Tomahawk sea-launched Cruise missile, first deployed in the Pacific in June of 1984, and described by Caspar Weinberger as "the cornerstone of our efforts to increase and diversify the striking power of the fleet." For the USSR to rid itself of the SLCM threat, retired U.S. admirals Elmo Zumwalt and Worth Bagley argue that "the Soviets would have to launch simultaneous attacks against the [nuclear] strike-capable ships dispersed widely over regional waters. It is an impossible task." Not being able to prevent nuclear retaliation from the sea, "Moscow cannot be expected to risk the use of nuclear weapons against our naval forces defending regional interests," the Navy maintains. The Cruise-carrying battleship of the Iowa Task Force could, for example, be used to reinforce the intervention of the Rapid Deployment Force in the Persian Gulf. To prevent the Soviets' northern fleet from moving into the Mediterranean to counter U.S. moves in the Persian Gulf, the Iowa Task Force could remain on station in the North Atlantic and confine the Soviets to the Norwegian Sea. The Iowa Task Force (like similar task forces armed with Cruise missiles based in California and Hawaii) would also serve as a mobile intervention fleet. The Iowa force could dodge from Iceland to the Indian Ocean; it could appear menacingly off the coast of Lebanon or Libya, supporting the Rapid Deployment Force; or it could "quarantine" some part of Africa.

Adm. James D. Watkins, now chief of naval operations and formerly commander of the Pacific fleet, told the U.S. Senate Armed Services Committee in March of 1982 that "Introduction of TLAM-N, the nuclear land-attack version of Tomahawk, will significantly increase the Pacific Fleet's theatre nuclear arsenal and provide the capability to strike land targets from survivable sea-based platforms." In effect, the SLCM is being sold as the ticket to regional nuclear superiority. Michael MacGuire of the Brookings Institution came to a similar conclusion: "It will improve the U.S. capability for military intervention in distant sea areas, for which there appears to be a growing political demand."

According to Pentagon theory, the USSR might not retaliate against a U.S. carrier that had just destroyed its forward units in Iran, for fear that the U.S. would then use the unique capabilities of its Cruise missiles to eliminate "surgically" all the bases, depots, command posts and reserves in Eastern Europe and Western Russia that support Soviet Middle Eastern theatre operations.

The Cruise missile, a one-time unwanted child of the American nuclear arsenal, has come a long way in Pentagon planning. As we'll see in Chapter 7, the Strategic Defense Initiative also promises to fit neatly into nuclear war-fighting plans.

Nuclear "Chicken"

The strategies of the nuclear arms race do not develop in a political vacuum. They arise from real policies and actual conflicts — on Caribbean beaches or in Mid-East cities. The most likely arena of superpower conflict is the Third World, and the most likely scenario for a nuclear war is the escalation of conflict in some designated strategic area of the world after one side fails to back down when its bluff is called.

During the Cuban missile crisis the world was incredibly lucky that President Kennedy backed down at the very last minute; Kennedy himself is quoted in

Theodore Sorensen's memoirs as saying that he felt there was a two out of five chance of a nuclear war. Extended deterrence is not a game that can be played forever. It is a high-risk gamble which in a time of attenuated crisis can transform threat into reality. A threat can be credible only so long; then it loses its force and must be refurbished to appear more menacing.

For this reason the United States is, essentially, waging a campaign to convince the Soviet Union that when America threatens the use of a nuclear weapon against the Soviets or against Soviet interests, it means it and is capable of carrying it out. The accompanying philosophy is provided by the likes of Colin Gray: "Washington should identify war aims that in the last resort would contemplate the destruction of Soviet political authority and the emergence of a post war world order compatible with Western values."

The American intent is surely not to trigger an actual full-scale nuclear war and all the horror and devastation that would entail. But U.S. strategic planners do have an objective they call "victory," meaning the power to organize the world to suit the interests of corporate America, and to rule without interference from the Soviet Union or from "Soviet-inspired" Third World regimes. They want what Sir Solly Zuckerman, the British Nobel laureate, has described as the best kind of victory — one in which the enemy surrenders to superior force without a shot being fired. Paul Nitze has compared the situation to "a game of chess. The atomic queens may never be brought into play; they may never actually take one of the opponent's pieces. But the position of the atomic queens may still have a decisive bearing on which side can safely advance a limited-war bishop or even a cold-war pawn."

The new pursuit of superiority in the face of continually modernizing forces, however, will result in prolonging reliance on nuclear threats in an era when such threats will be vastly more dangerous than before — more likely to be challenged and carried out and more likely to be suicidal as well as genocidal.

Richard Barnet, one of the most astute critics of American foreign policy, points out how dangerous current strategy is in a period when nuclear weapons cannot be relied upon to "manage" crises or to compensate for local military or political weaknesses, and when nuclear threats, whether conveyed by word or deed, produce not a properly cowed Soviet leadership but a vengeful, nervous and error-prone Politburo:

> Having achieved rough parity with the U.S. in military power, their national-security managers are now much more likely to think like their U.S. counterparts: "We can't afford to back down and be exposed as a pitiful, helpless giant." Thus the happy accident that the world has survived the first thirty-five years of the nuclear era is unimpressive evidence that we can avoid nuclear war in the coming era, for world power relationships are changing faster than we can comprehend and the arms race has become an entirely new game. The impending new stage of the military competition is likely to make the world of the 1970s look in retrospect like a Quaker village.

Many years ago, the famous political economist Joseph Schumpeter analyzed the foreign policy of ancient Rome in terms eerily appropriate to our times. The Romans, he said, pursued a policy that

> pretended to aspire to peace but unerringly generated war; the policy of continual preparation for war; the

policy of meddlesome interventionism. There was no corner of the known world where some interest was not alleged to be in danger or under actual attack. If the interests were not Roman they were those of Rome's allies, and if Rome had no allies then allies would be invented. And when it was utterly impossible to contrive such an interest, why then it was the national honour that had been assaulted.

The fight was always invested with an aura of legality. Rome was always being attacked by evil-minded neighbours, always fighting for breathing space. The whole world was pervaded by a host of enemies and it was manifestly Rome's duty to guard against their indubitably aggressive designs.

Like Rome, the United States is mortally wounding itself by the very policies it pursues in the name of strength. By committing itself to fully integrating nuclear weapons into its general foreign policy objectives, and by presenting nuclear war as a viable alternative, the United States has increased its own security by increasing the likelihood of a world-wide nuclear war. To issue first-use warnings in a world so loaded with nuclear weapons which both threaten and invite pre-emption is to truly play Russian roulette.

4
The European Theatre

An intercontinental exchange and the escalation of a Third World showdown between the superpowers are two of the major nuclear scenarios. The third is a battle for Europe.

Europe is bristling with Soviet SS-20 missiles and the American Pershing II and Cruise missiles which, supposedly, were put in place to deter the USSR from using the SS-20s. But the decision to deploy the Cruise and Pershing II actually had very little to do with deterrence.

The SS-20 Threat

In the West, the SS-20 deployment beginning in the late 1970s was perceived as representing a "new threat" in the European theatre and one that ominously seemed to imply political intimidation — a sort of "Pax Sovietica." A typical complaint was that of former Canadian Deputy Minister of Defense Buzz Nixon, who argued: "Not only do these missiles constitute a dire military threat but their very presence creates an oppressive sword of Damocles hanging over the heads of West Europeans in the conduct of all their relations with the Soviet Union." The European peace movement too was unequivocally opposed to SS-20 deployment.

There is no question that the West was right to be concerned by the rapid growth of Soviet SS-20s. Technically and strategically, the SS-20s are far more lethal than the SS-4 and SS-5 missiles they replaced. The SS-20 is mobile, while its predecessors were stationary. The SS-4 and SS-5 were large, cumbersome, liquid-fueled missiles with very slow reaction times (requiring several hours to prepare for firing). Arranged in close groups and usually unprotected, they were exceedingly vulnerable.

Technically, the SS-4 was well on its way to being a candidate for a museum. The rocket drew heavily from the technology of the German V-2; twelve tractors with special trailers, manned by a crew of about twenty, were required to transport, erect and fire one weapon. Once in flight, the SS-4 corrected its course with the primitive and highly fallible device of external fins.

The SS-5 was a bit more sophisticated. Its trajectory was controlled by vanes acting on the motor exhaust, and it had a range nearly twice that of the SS-4. Both missiles were poor deterrents however, thanks to their vulnerability to a NATO pre-emptive attack and the long lead time necessary to fuel them. In all likelihood they would have had to be the first nuclear weapons used in a European conflict and consequently were highly destabilizing.

The SS-20 is two generations ahead of the SS-4 and SS-5 in every respect. It is fueled by solid propellant, which is more reliable and manageable than liquid fuel, and it is armed with three MIRVs rather than a single warhead. Each MIRV has a yield ten times that of the Hiroshima bomb — sufficient to devastate any one of the European cities against which they are aimed. (Because the SS-20, like the Pershing, is a rapid reload-refire system, the actual number of warheads is more than three per missile.) The SS-20 has a greater range, of nearly 3,100 miles, and it can be moved about on truck-like vehicles. And the SS-20 is six times more accurate than the SS-4.

It is estimated that about two-thirds of the SS-20s are targeted on Western Europe, the rest on China. Any SS-20 based to the west of the Urals could strike any part of Western Europe, including England.

While there is no denying the horror of the SS-20's firepower, many experts believe that the move from the SS-4 and SS-5 missiles (which had been deployed since 1959 and 1961, respectively) to the SS-20 was in part a defensive one, an effort to make Soviet forces less vulnerable to attack. European weapons researchers Sverre Lodgaard and Per Berg state:

> For intelligence services and military experts, the introduction of the SS-20 was ... no surprise; on the contrary, it was technically overdue ... it represented no radical departure in doctrine.... The decision may have seemed an easy one to make, and to a large extent it may have been reduced to a matter of military-bureaucratic automaticity, without much consideration of its impact on international affairs.

Though official doctrine would argue otherwise, analyses of the SS-20 deployment prior to the NATO Cruise and Pershing II modernization supported the view that there was no new "threat." In June of 1979, a NATO review described the introduction of the SS-20 as "non-dramatic." In its publication *Military Balance 1979-80*, Britain's prestigious Institute for Strategic Studies summarized establishment attitudes. From this perspective, 260 SS-20 missiles were seen as an acceptable component of Moscow's counter to America's forward-based systems (land- and carrier-based nuclear-armed fighter bombers plus NATO-assigned submarines) and British and French forces. Only if deployment proceeded beyond 260 would parity be endangered. (By the summer of 1985, the Soviets had deployed approximately 440 SS-20 missiles — exceeding a one-for-one ratio in replacing the SS-4s and SS-5s.) As noted by Raymond Garthoff, former U.S. State Department expert on the Soviet military, "It seems highly likely that, in the Soviets' place, U.S. and NATO military and political leaders would have done exactly the same thing, and would have considered such a modernization programme as fully justified." Many others, including McGeorge Bundy, special assistant for national security affairs to Presidents Kennedy and Johnson, have noted that the SS-20 does not give the Soviet Union any significant nuclear capability against Western Europe that it did not have before a single SS-20 was deployed. The military value of the new Soviet missiles is marginal given the vast size of Soviet intermediate-range nuclear forces.

It is also significant that the SS-20, by virtue of its medium range and geographical deployment, cannot be targeted against American strategic weapons — unless, of course, the U.S. places such weapons in Europe! Consequently, the former director of the International Institute for Strategic Studies, Christopher Bertram, has described the comparison between the SS-20 and the Pershing II and Cruise as "analyticallly dubious."

While the SS-20 does not shatter the military balance in Europe, it certainly is an acceleration of the arms race, and by virtue of its counter military potential, fits easily into nuclear war-fighting scenarios. Whether the SS-20 gives the USSR superiority in Europe is quite another question, one that is obscured by arts of deception practised by both superpowers.

The Counting War

At a press conference on January 20, 1982, President Reagan made the following somewhat unsyntactical observation: "We claim that to continue to stand there with [the Soviets] having enough warheads to literally wipe out every population centre in Western Europe, with no deterrent on our side, and the NATO allies recognize this, and we have said at their request that we will provide a deterrent." The assertion that NATO lacks a deterrent for the SS-20 has been widely repeated. One of Canada's foremost military analysts, John Gellner, editor of *Canadian Defence Quarterly*, argued: "At present, there is no equivalent in the NATO arsenal — and thus no deterrent — to intermediate-range nuclear missiles stationed in European Russia."

These comments are based, however, on the use of completely artificial definitions. They compare only land-based intermediate-range nuclear forces (those weapons with a range greater than 620 miles but less than intercontinental strategic weapons). Not surprisingly, the result is that NATO, before Pershing II and Cruise missile deployment, is put at a disadvantage of about 1,000 warheads to zero. But NATO has substantial intermediate-range nuclear weapons — they simply aren't land-based. These include F-11 and Vulcan nuclear-capable bombers, the British Polaris, the French "independent" nuclear arsenal and the American nuclear-armed Poseidon submarines. Each Poseidon submarine carries enough multiple-warhead missiles to destroy all the major cities in the Soviet Union. Retired Maj. Gen. William T. Fairbourn of the U.S.

Marine Corps has said that "NATO had quite wisely deployed untargetable submarines — not land-based missiles — as a response to the Soviet intermediate [land-based] missiles aimed at Europe. It is simply wrong to say that we have nothing to counter the SS-20s." Admiral Falls, a Canadian who is former chairman of NATO's military committee, appreciated the importance of the European sea-based deterrent: "Western politicians tend to forget the importance of submarine-launched missiles which have an enormous deterrent capability and which should force leaders to think again about the need for new ground-launched missiles."

Another layer of confusion is added by the question of whether the French and British nuclear arsenals (of approximately 300 warheads each) should be counted as part of NATO's total intermediate-range nuclear weapons. The U.S. argues that they should not because these forces are not formally under NATO's command. Neither France nor the U.K. wants to have its missiles counted in the Euro-strategic negotiations as this would add pressure on them not to increase their nuclear forces. Modernization plans in France and the U.K. could raise the number of warheads targeted against the Soviet Union by an additional 2,000 before the mid 1990s. Trident II alone will increase the number of British warheads to almost 900, roughly equal to the total number of SS-20 warheads currently targeted on Europe.

There seems to be a good deal of hypocrisy in the American arguments on this matter. Imagine that Brazil and Mexico were allied with the Soviet Union, that they had nuclear forces, on a scale similar to French and British forces, targeted on the United States. Say that Brazil had its own force expansion program and

Mexico had contracted to buy a follow-on version of the SS-20 for deployment in the 1990s, that the Mexican forces were assigned to a Soviet commander for targeting purposes. Would the U.S. government not want to take them into account in negotiations? Princeton political scientist Richard H. Ullman has observed: "For years, all the Western governments have had a stock answer to the question: when is a missile not a missile? The answer: when it is marked with the Union Jack or the Tricolor."

In terms of the plain U.S.-USSR balance, both superpowers have put forward calculations of the systems they believe relevant to negotiations on intermediate nuclear forces in Europe. Not surprisingly, they came up with dramatically different figures in a 1981 comparison. The differences between the American and Soviet versions are less over the numbers of each weapon system than over which systems should be included.

The basic construction of the Soviet position is bogus. To give but two examples: the USSR claims an existing equality of aircraft and missiles in Europe, at just under 1,000 apiece. However, it can only construct this equality by disregarding its own counting rules when they become inconvenient. The Soviets impose a geographical restriction to exclude from negotiations their own aircraft and systems facing China (systems which could be moved to face Western Europe in a crisis), yet they wish to include U.S. FB-111 aircraft plus A-6 and A-7 aircraft or carriers, both based outside of the Soviet guidelines area. The USSR's calculation includes the Pershing I, which has a range well under 620 miles. Then the Soviets turn right around and do not count a hundred or so SS-12s and SS-22s, which have ranges considerably greater than the Pershing I.

With methods such as these the Soviets arrived at a rough parity in weapons: 986 NATO to 975 Warsaw Pact.

The United States also manipulated the figures to suit its purposes. The American tally of 3,825 Soviet weapons vs. 560 American — hence, a six to one ratio — excluded French and English systems and shorter-range American missiles, while it included all the Soviet Badger, Blinder, Fencer and Flogger aircraft, whose equivalents had been ignored when counting American weapons.

The most respected and impartial accounting of the nuclear arms race comes from two independent military research institutes: the London-based International Institute for Strategic Studies (IISS) and the Stockholm International Peace Research Institute (SIPRI). Each of these bodies has found the American and Soviet calculations of the intermediate-range nuclear arms race to be equally inaccurate and almost totally self-serving. According to both SIPRI and IISS evaluations, the Soviet Union (before NATO deployment of Pershing II and Cruise missiles) had a superiority in European intermediate-range nuclear weapons in the range of two to one. The Soviets enjoyed such a Euro-missile advantage well before the SS-20 deployments. However, NATO has always had a massive deterrent outside these counting categories since U.S. strategic forces reinforce European theatre missiles. The Soviet advantage in intermediate-range nuclear weapons originally balanced the U.S. lead in intercontinental missiles. While waiting for their own intercontinental missiles, the Soviets held Western Europe hostage. But if a Soviet first strike should occur in Europe today, the existing NATO forces would be capable, without the Pershing II and Cruise missiles, of inflicting unacceptable damage on the Soviet Union. In fact, U.S. Secretary of State Vance testified to Congress that NATO's nuclear capability was quite adequate regardless of the SS-20. Others — like former Defense Secretary McNamara and British Field Marshall Lord Carver — argue that the NATO capability is grossly in excess of deterrence requirements. One analysis, by Dieter Lutz of the Institute for Peace Research and Security Policy, suggests that NATO's firepower requirements are consistently overestimated, because the concentration of Soviet infrastructure and population in the easily-attacked European part of the country is not taken into account. Lutz concludes that even after a Soviet first strike, NATO (excluding the American strategic arsenal) would still have 259 MIRVed warheads of 50 kilotons, 62 single warheads of 200 kilotons, and 26 warheads of one megaton, or more than enough to destroy the thirty largest cities in the USSR and about forty per cent of its industry. The point, of course, is not that the Soviet Union's Euromissiles are thereby made acceptable, but rather that the demand for European parity is political, not military. NATO's deterrent, in other words, is already adequate.

Rationale of the NATO Decision

Where then did the demand for the Cruise and Pershing II originate? The popular version of the Intermediate Nuclear Forces story is that the Soviets surprised the West with their SS-20 build-up; the Europeans then asked the U.S. for an equivalent land-based component, and the U.S. grudgingly agreed to deploy it on European territory. The true story is much more complex, bringing into play the impetus provided by both American doctrine and weapon-systems advances.

There are a good number of developments in the 1970s that show the European Cruise to be American-inspired. The United States had been funding research and development of the Pershing II and GLCM since the early 1970s, long before SS-20 deployment began. In the mid-1970s the U.S. Department of Defense commissioned a study by the Stanford Research Institute on political attitudes in Europe toward the introduction of new nuclear weapons. The study concluded:

> Efforts must be made ... to involve larger segments of the governmental bureaucracies in Europe in the discussions on nuclear weapons modernization and on the capabilities of the new systems, and to involve European political leaders in the dialogue on NATO force modernization to an even greater extent than heretofor.

The European members of NATO who first expressed an interest in the Cruise missile in the mid-1970s had been sold on its attributes by weapons manufacturers in the United States. As Hans Eberhard, the top weapons buyer in the West German defense ministry from 1975 to 1981, remembers, "The U.S. manufacturers badly wanted a European endorsement for the Cruise missile. We got good advice that it was a valuable weapon."

NATO's High Level Group, which undertook to study the need for new Euro-missiles, was established in October of 1977. A year previously, President Ford had announced that he had approved the proposal to start engineering development of the GLCM. With a range of 1,550 miles, the GLCMs would have no obvious targets if stationed in the U.S.; logic suggested they were intended for deployment in Western Europe

112 Misguided Missiles

and perhaps, though less likely, Northeast Asia. In May of 1977, also prior to the HLG deliberations, the Pentagon circulated a document to its allies asking them whether they were still confident that the four Poseidon missile submarines allocated to NATO provided adequate links between Europe and the U.S. strategic nuclear arsenal. This paper came at a very sensitive time in NATO politics. To cite an American general quoted in the *London Times*, "Anyone who believes that the call for the missiles originated in Europe must believe in Santa Claus."

In October of 1977, German Chancellor Helmut Schmidt made his famous speech expressing concern about the impact of the SALT process upon European security. Many Europeans saw in SALT signs that the United States, not surprisingly, assigned a lower priority to the strategic problems of Europe than to the American-Soviet relationship. Suspicions were aroused by the apparent readiness of the U.S. to tolerate Soviet Backfire bombers and SS-20 missiles, provided they could not be used against the continental United States. Schmidt argued that the achievement of strategic (intercontinental) nuclear parity by the superpowers increased the significance of the disparities between East and West in European theatre nuclear and conventional forces. He maintained that the "principle of parity," or equal level of armaments, between East and West "must apply to all weapons" — not only those in the U.S. and the USSR, for which SALT provided, but also those in Western and Eastern Europe. It has been reported that Chancellor Schmidt consulted closely with U.S. officials on the contents of his speech.

The NATO decision stemmed as much from European mistrust of the American guarantee to use nuclear weapons to defend Western Europe as from Western concern over Soviet deployments of the SS-20. As British scholar Michael Howard put it, the underlying problem was reassurance of the West more than deterrence of the East. The fears of some European governments that the U.S. strategic nuclear deterrent was being "de-coupled" from the defense of Europe had to be allayed.

The Carter administration, which came to power in 1977, was largely opposed to the deployment of the Cruise missile because its small size was considered an insurmountable obstacle to arms control verification. But the administration's resistance was finally worn down by European threats to withhold support for SALT II, then in the final stages of negotiation, unless more modern intermediate-range nuclear weapons such as the Cruise were forthcoming. According to Raymond Garthoff, a diplomat in the Carter administration, high-level members of the principal Western European governments were told that Washington did not see the need for a new deployment to reinforce deterrence, but was prepared to proceed if the Allies believed it necessary. After a British, German, French and American consensus was reached in a summit meeting at Guadeloupe in January of 1979, the United States vigorously took the lead in organizing the alliance. Indeed, some Western European NATO nations have privately complained that the United States "railroaded" the decision. In his study of "modernization," Gregory Treverton, staff member for Europe on the U.S. National Security Council, noted "The European allies had no formal veto in the process of decision making of the HLG [High Level Group].... The United States left little doubt at least from the beginning of 1979 onwards of the direction it wanted NATO to take."

The Reagan administration inherited the Cruise and Pershing II decision but was less than enthusiastic about deploying the missiles. Richard Perle, the hawkish congressional staffer who would soon become assistant secretary of defense for international security policy, questioned "the cost benefit wisdom" of the deployments. Perle has more recently acknowledged that the missiles were of questionable military value and that if the decision had to be made again he would oppose deployment. Fred Ikle, another long-time hawk who joined the administration as under-secretary of defense for policy, feared that getting the West Europeans to accept the missiles would cause more trouble within the alliance than the missiles were worth.

Why was the Reagan administration so unenthusiastic about the Pershing II and ground-launched Cruise missile? After all, their deployment was seen by some military critics as a way of circumventing the SALT II Treaty and helping re-establish U.S. strategic superiority. Under Reagan, however, the United States had fewer qualms about ignoring the SALT II provisions and letting the treaty die a quiet death. The Pershing and Cruise missiles were dispensable, and their loss could be more than compensated for in a new strategic build-up.

Flexible Response

Whatever the attitude of the European allies may have been, Pentagon doctrine evolved in the late 1970s in favour of modernizing the nuclear deterrent in Europe. This gave the Cruise a mighty boost. The NATO nuclear doctrine, adopted in 1967, of "flexible response" — of escalation dominance, essentially — requires a "spectrum" of nuclear delivery systems to provide

NATO with a full range of "flexible options" short of "massive nuclear retaliation" in the event of war. Flexible response also demands that NATO be prepared to consider the option of escalating to a higher level of nuclear violence in response to a Soviet attack, even if this ultimately means drawing in America's strategic nuclear arsenal.

The first rung of the flexible response doctrine's ladder of escalation is occupied by conventional weapons. On the second step up are short-range ("battlefield") nuclear weapons. The third rung is medium-range nuclear weapons, and at the top of the ladder are intercontinental missiles.

Rapid advances in Soviet military technology encouraged NATO officials to believe, by the mid-1970s, that there was a gap in the spectrum. Existing American and British bombers assigned to NATO in Europe were said to be becoming obsolete, unable to penetrate Warsaw Pact air defenses and vulnerable on the ground to pre-emptive attack. This gap put NATO's entire posture into question; the threat was no longer convincing. And the gap faced the SS-20s on the Soviet ladder.

Senior NATO officials contended that Poseidon submarine missiles under NATO command were too inaccurate and inflexible to fill the gap. The "hard-target kill potential" of the SS-20 warheads was said by NATO planners to give the Soviets an option for a first-strike attack that the less accurate Poseidon warheads lack. The Poseidon is incapable of limited attacks on military targets, both because its low-yield, low-accuracy warheads are more suitable for city-industrial targeting, and because any such attack by a Poseidon would not be limited (since post-launch vulnerability would necessitate the simultaneous firing of all sixteen of its missiles with a total of 160 warheads). The argument was that NATO could be faced with what former U.S. Defense Secretary Harold Brown called a "cruel choice" not to retaliate with Poseidons. The fact that the SS-20 could supposedly be used selectively led to fears that the Soviets possessed escalation dominance in the European theatre, enjoying superiority not only in conventional forces but also on the upper rungs of the nuclear ladder.

But it seems implausible that SS-20s could ever be used in a limited, pre-emptive attack against Western military targets, for the missile's accuracy is too poor and its warheads too large for such a strike to be distinguishable from an all-out nuclear onslaught. Yet NATO hypotheses are based on a pre-emptive attack. McGeorge Bundy remarked:

> When it is carefully considered, the proposal to deploy Cruise and Pershing II is neither necessary nor desirable for the safety of the Alliance.... The SS-20 did not and does not give the Soviet Union any nuclear capability against Europe alone that it did not have in overflowing quantity before a single SS-20 was deployed, and on this quite basic point, the simplistic analysis of some nuclear planners, in NATO and elsewhere, has been deeply misleading to their political superiors....

Mobility and a shorter reaction time have made the Soviet SS-20s a more formidable retaliatory nuclear force without, however, giving them the capacity to strike first.

In the minds of some NATO strategists, this strengthened deterrent — which decreases NATO's nuclear threat — posed a problem further down the escalation ladder. Believing the Russians capable of attacking Europe with superior conventional forces, they looked with dismay on the possibility that the Soviet SS-20s had effectively neutralized the West's threat to respond to such an invasion with nuclear weapons. Western Europe still had a credible deterrent to Soviet nuclear weapons but no longer had (if it ever had) a credible nuclear threat to conventional Soviet forces. The wording in the 1979 NATO communiqué on "modernization" is instructive:

> Soviet improvements in Theatre Nuclear Forces have prompted serious concern in the Alliance, for such Soviet superiority could undermine the stability of intercontinental systems and cast doubt on the credibility of the Alliance's deterrent strategy by highlighting the gap in the spectrum of NATO's available nuclear response to aggression....

This passage does not say that SS-20s are a new threat to NATO; they are only a threat to the way NATO nuclear strategy "works." Such nuances are of major significance but have been lost in subsequent debate. The SS-20 only makes inescapable what Western European leaders have known for years: that in an era of strategic nuclear parity it is no longer realistic to offset Soviet conventional military strength with nuclear weapons. In that sense, the SS-20 is intimidating. But the NATO nuclear option was a military crutch, and repairing the crutch does not cure the invalid. (The notion of conventional superiority giving the Soviets the freedom to overrun Europe will be returned to later in this chapter.)

For NATO planners, the Cruise and Pershing II would re-establish the seamless web of deterrence that the SS-20 was splitting apart. This view, which prevailed in NATO defense circles in the late 1970s, persuaded the Carter administration — against its initial better judgment — that Europeans would feel secure only when the United States could dominate all the rungs of the ladder.

The SS-20 only started to figure prominently in NATO discussions after it had been generally agreed which new missiles were required. As a NATO report says:

> The HLG deliberations initially concerned the deficiencies of NATO's own capabilities. However, in the public discussion, attention increasingly focused on the SS-20.... The overemphasis on the SS-20 was perhaps inevitable because it is easier to discuss publicly the need for LRTNF [long-range theatre nuclear force] modernization by pointing to visible Soviet capabilities than by explaining somewhat esoteric NATO doctrine.

The "esoteric NATO doctrine" is, of course, the doctrine of controlled escalation and limited nuclear war. Before long the "Cruise and Pershing are a response to SS-20" formula was becoming orthodox political wisdom. Yet the real inspiration of the modernization is not denied. General Rogers, NATO Supreme Allied Commander (Europe) has said that "even without the SS-20, NATO was moving towards Pershing II and GLCMs by 1978...." Simon Lunn, advisor to the president of the European Parliament, has also shown how "NATO's modernization requirements were not related to the number of SS-20s deployed."

The "Two-Track" Policy

From the preceding, we can see that there was considerable momentum for new NATO missiles in Europe by the time NATO announced its "two-track" policy in December of 1979. One track was an offer to the USSR to start negotiations on limiting intermediate-range nuclear missiles in the European theatre. The second was the decision to deploy 464 ground-launched Cruise missiles and 108 Pershing II missiles beginning in December of 1983 unless the negotiations had produced an agreement. In this modernization scheme, all the Pershing IIs and 96 of the GLCMs were to be deployed in West Germany. Britain would receive 160 GLCMs, Italy 112, and Belgium and the Netherlands 48 each. The two tracks were announced in the same communiqué as "parallel and complementary approaches in order to avert an arms race in Europe caused by the Soviet build-up, yet to preserve the viability of NATO's strategy of deterrence and defense."

Canada has been a consistent supporter of the NATO modernization decision. Prime Minister Trudeau advocated a firm NATO stance to "show the Soviet Union we can match them, gun for gun, if necessary." His argument was that only American deployment of new missiles would force the Soviets to back down and remove the SS-20s.

Trudeau was not alone in finding the arms-for-disarmament logic of the two-track decision sound. Yet many observers felt that the U.S. arms control offer was a dead letter, designed to win support for deployment from unenthusiastic ministers in weak coalition governments, such as in Belgium and Holland, and to satisfy the peace movement in Western Europe. The offer, after all, ran completely counter to the reasoning behind the deployment of the Cruise and Pershing II missiles.

"Two-Track" Talks

In November of 1981, the INF talks opened in Geneva. Both the United States and the USSR adopted extreme positions. Out of one corner came the Soviets with the proposal to add no more missiles following their build-up of more than 200 SS-20s with three warheads each, provided that the West did not go ahead with the Cruise and Pershing II. Out of the opposite corner, President Reagan announced his "zero option." Reagan proposed that all land-based intermediate-range missiles be eliminated; the United States would forego deployment of ground-launched Cruise and Pershing II missiles in exchange for the Soviet Union's dismantling of all SS-4, SS-5 and SS-20 missiles in Europe.

As lopsided as the Soviet proposal, which merely confirmed a fait accompli, the U.S. offer focused only on the intermediate-range land-based missiles in which the Soviets had concentrated their strength. But it left untouched systems of Western strength. The restriction of the negotiations to land-based intermediate-range missiles made it clear from the beginning that deployment of some new NATO missiles was considered a foregone conclusion, for the U.S. had had no missiles in the intermediate-range category since 1963, leaving the USSR with a virtual monopoly.

Essentially, the Soviets were asked to dismantle all of their land-based INF systems; to permit the U.S. to retain both its European-based Poseidon submarines and all of its forward-based nuclear-capable aircraft; to allow the U.S. to develop new sea-launched Cruise missiles; and to allow Britain and France to retain and modernize their INF assets. A NATO assembly report accurately referred to "the objective of recognizing the zero option as a desirable but implausible goal [whose purpose] is to place the responsibility for NATO modernization on the Soviet Union." The proposal was so skewed that it seemed designed more for grandstanding than for negotiating. Even Reagan's first secretary of state, Alexander Haig, understood that the zero option was not negotiable:

> It was absurd to expect the Soviets to dismantle an existing force of 1,100 warheads, which they had already put into the field at a cost of billions of rubles, in exchange for a promise from the United States not to deploy a missile force that we had not yet begun to build and that had aroused such violent controversy in Western Europe.

General Rowny, appointed chief U.S. strategic arms negotiator in 1981, when asked at a congressional hearing why the U.S. had opened talks on intermediate-range weapons, replied:

> In the interest of getting some GLCMs and Pershing IIs deployed in Europe the Administration, as had the past Administration, agreed to a twin track approach. It is proper to live up to our commitment of getting modernized forces deployed in Europe. The Administration considered it good for Alliance solidarity to open INF talks at an early date…"

Richard Burt of the State Department is reported to have said of the negotiations to his staff: "The purpose of this whole exercise is maximum political advantage. It's not arms control we're engaged in, it's alliance management." Not surprisingly, the Soviets dismissed the proposal out of hand.

Pershing II and Cruise Deployment

With the ritual of arms control negotiations out of the way, the deployment of Pershing II and Cruise missiles in Western Europe could go ahead, introducing a new, greater and qualitatively different danger of nuclear war in the European theatre. The Pershing II, though deployed in much smaller numbers than the Cruise, is of special significance because of its utility for the American "decapitation" strategy. Its speed and accuracy give it this potential. The missile could reach missile silos and command and control installations (constructed several hundred feet underground) in the western part of the Soviet Union with very little warning — under ten minutes. In the words of John Pike of the Federation of American Scientists, this gives "the people in the Kremlin just enough time to say 'Oh shit'." As for accuracy, the SS-20 is estimated to have a CEP (circular error probability, a measure of accuracy) of about 440 yards; the Pershing II warhead can be delivered to within about 44 yards of its target. The Pershing is a formidable threat to the highly centralized (hence more vulnerable) Soviet command system, a threat not matched by the much less accurate SS-20. And it is not unlikely that improvements can be made to allow a new generation of Pershings to reach Moscow, making the threat even greater.

Moreover, Gen. Richard Ellis, former commander in chief of the U.S. Strategic Air Command, has said:

> Those weapons [Pershing II and Cruise] provide an offensive capability that [the Soviets] cannot duplicate. By that I mean, we would be able to strike the Russian homeland, the capital, with weapons based in Europe ... whereas they cannot reach the United States with their SS-20 or other theatre-type missiles.

More particularly, Pershing II missiles would threaten Soviet strategic weapons while SS-20s do not threaten American strategic weapons.

What is the Soviet attitude to this danger? Paul Warnke has argued that

> Pershing IIs can be considered as best suited for a decapitating attack. Although the ground-launched Cruise missiles are much slower, their reputed accuracy is comparable. In combination with other planned American systems, such as the MX and the Trident II, or D-5 submarine-launched ballistic missile, they can be seen by the Soviets as contributing to a first-strike potential.

The Pershing's short flight time makes launch-on-warning responses all too compelling, at a time when even the relatively more sophisticated U.S. warning systems continue occasionally to read the rising of the moon and flocks of Canada geese as incoming missiles or bombers. Although Helmut Schmidt is credited with the speech calling for the deployment of Pershings, less attention has been paid to his later admission, that he had no idea at the time of their speed, or the threat they would represent to the Soviets.

In sum, the effect of the Pershing II and Cruise missiles in Europe will be to increase domestic and international tensions, heighten the odds that nuclear weapons will be used if war begins, encourage hair-trigger launching plans and pre-emptive strategies and stimulate new Soviet deployments closer to U.S. borders. Consequently, the thirteen "Generals for Peace" (all retired NATO generals) made this appeal to the United States: "American first-strike weapons on the doorstep of the Soviet Union are the most appropriate fuse for touching off a nuclear world war. Americans, we beseech you: Do not deploy Pershing II and Cruise missiles in Europe. For the sake of humankind, don't do it."

Sacrificing Europe

Some participants in the European peace movement have charged that the new missiles free the U.S. to conduct nuclear war against the Soviet Union with Europe as the battleground. The Pershing II and Cruise do enable the U.S. to devise scenarios for limited nuclear war that do not involve the continental United States, and the Pershing II in particular allows plans for a disarming first strike. The Soviet Union, unable to retaliate with similar high-accuracy, low-yield weapons against U.S. territory, may respond by turning its less accurate weapons against Western Europe. In this case, Western Europe would be the hostage and eventually the victim of an American nuclear attack on the European part of the USSR. A comparable situation existed before the advent of Soviet intercontinental forces, when Soviet intermediate-range nuclear weapons were deployed toward Europe to compensate for U.S. strategic nuclear superiority.

However, one reason originally put forward on behalf of Pershing II and Cruise deployment was the need to clearly link the defense of Western Europe and the U.S. strategic deterrent. Pierre Trudeau, for one, had his doubts about the strength of the bond: "Do you think the President of the United States, in answer to an overrunning of Europe by conventional Soviet forces, will want to start World War III, and atomic war?" In a rare moment of frankness, Henry Kissinger told the NATO allies that the United States would hardly risk New York and Washington to defend, say, Hamburg or Berlin against an attack directed at the U.S. Exactly because the Europeans sensed the limitations of America's commitment, it was necessary to install the missiles in Western Europe.

While the general belief in Europe is that Pershing II and the Cruise can deter Soviet aggression by threatening to trigger superpower Armageddon, the Americans believe that the missiles provide deterrence by enabling NATO to control war short of superpower Armageddon. When the United States possessed clear nuclear superiority, it could be argued that this plan to use Europe as the theatre had a certain plausibility — or "credibility," to use the favoured term — because it was at least possible to imagine that if the Soviet Union was faced with a nuclear attack in Europe it would refrain from responding in kind. European NATO governments are still trying to sustain the myth. In this regard American arms negotiator Paul Warnke observed that "the only contrary theory that I have heard is that the Soviets would be more apt to regard it more leniently if they were hit by a warhead from West Germany than if they were hit by one from South Dakota. I rather doubt that that is the case."

For the same reason that led Henry Kissinger to recognize that a U.S. president is unlikely to initiate the use of American-based strategic nuclear weapons against the USSR, so a president would be unlikely to launch American-controlled missiles from Europe against Russia. But European governments continue to cling to the assumption that the U.S.'s willingness to use nuclear weapons would be significantly influenced by where they were based. The only reason why European-based weapons might be more likely to be used in the course of a European war is that the U.S.

might feel pressure to launch them if the invading forces were about to destroy or capture them. But as George Ball, under-secretary of state during the Kennedy and Johnson administrations, has remarked: "In facing the decision to fire nuclear missiles, I do not believe any American President would push the button just because the missiles might be overrun." Herbert York, a former director of research at the Pentagon, points out the consequences of this myth-making: "NATO's plans for the defense of Europe are centred on an awesome bluff. The current happy political stability in Europe ... is being bought by placing at risk the entire future of the continent and its people."

The Euro-missiles are said to be necessary to fill a gap in the ladder of escalation on which flexible response is based. Soviet SS-20s are said to have caused this gap. If the use of medium-range weapons is seen as a clearly demarcated phase in this escalation ladder, then the possibility of a non-intercontinental (limited) nuclear war is seemingly accepted. But the missiles would be targeted at the Soviet Union, and Soviet leaders have made it clear that they would consider the firing of the Euro-missiles a strategic attack, inviting Soviet retaliation not only against Western Europe but also against the United States.

There may, of course, be a discrepancy between Soviet rhetoric and behaviour, and the Soviets may seek to limit a nuclear exchange as much as possible. It is only wishful thinking on the part of the Americans, however, to believe that the USSR would tacitly agree to leave the U.S. mainland unscathed while its own most densely populated and industrialized region, containing a large proportion of its military installations, was being destroyed. Only if the U.S.-NATO missiles were targeted west of the Soviet Union — i.e., against Eastern Europe and excluding Russia — would there be a remote possibility that Moscow would not launch its missiles at the United States.

Presidents Carter and Reagan have claimed that "limited" or protracted nuclear war would prevent a global holocaust. "Limited," in American parlance, however, would mean that "only" Europe would be destroyed. The nearly unanimous conclusion of those who have studied this issue is that a nuclear war could not be controlled in this manner. The British Atlantic Committee, a London-based group of conservative defense experts, has said that the notion of defending Western Europe by "controlled step-by-step escalation" — starting with conventional weapons and moving gradually up the scale from battlefield to strategic nuclear weapons — is "impractical nonsense."

Unless and until NATO moves to the posture of deploying nuclear weapons exclusively to serve a simple, limited, but vital purpose — that is, deterring the use or threatened use of an adversary's nuclear weapon — it will be difficult to find any means to reduce the potential for nuclear escalation from battlefield nuclear weapons to theatre nuclear weapons to strategic nuclear weapons. The conviction that a nuclear war could be fought and won in Europe, or anywhere, is the same twisted logic as that used by the U.S. commander in Vietnam who argued that his troops had to destroy the village in order to save it. Given the increased knowledge of the effects of using even a small number of nuclear warheads, and the context of a densely populated central Europe, the destruction would be unimaginable. Morton Halperin, former U.S. deputy assistant secretary of defense, sums up the present predicament: "NATO doctrine is that we fight with conventional forces until we are losing, then we fight with tactical nuclear weapons until we are losing, then we will blow up the world."

The Warsaw Pact Conventional Threat and NATO Responses

Despite the spectre of a European holocaust, American planners use the threat of nuclear destruction to deter not only nuclear, but also conventional attack. This has been the practice since the first days of the Cold War, and to this day, NATO refuses to adopt a "no-first-use" pledge, claiming that the comparative weakness of its conventional forces requires that nuclear weapons be used to defend against — and thus to deter — a conventional attack by Warsaw Pact troops.

The assumption that the Soviets are eager to invade and administer the countries of Western Europe, while mildly plausible thirty years ago, today seems almost absurd to many critics of NATO policies. Since it was only forty years ago that Germany ruled France, and since half of Europe today consists of conquered nations, there is certainly a legitimate question of defense. Yet the European standoff of the past thirty-five years shows that no political objective would justify the risks of undertaking large-scale military activity in Western Europe. Why should the Soviets, who are increasingly unable to control Eastern Europe effectively, try to bite off Western Europe? George Kennan, former U.S. ambassador to the USSR and an early architect of American Cold War policy, has remarked:

> I can conceive that there might be certain European regions, outside the limits of their present hegemony, where they would be happy, for defensive purposes,

to have some sort of military control, if such control could be acquired safely and easily, without severe disruption of international stability; but it is a far cry from this to the assumption that they would be disposed to invade any of these areas out of the blue, in peacetime, at the cost of unleashing another world war.

The most sophisticated opponents of a NATO no-first-use nuclear declaration do not envision a direct Soviet invasion of Western Europe with conventional weapons, but a kind of military diplomacy by which political concessions would be required of European governments because they lacked the ability to defend themselves.

In either case, one must ask whether the Warsaw Pact really enjoys conventional superiority. The balance of conventional forces between the Warsaw Pact and NATO is complex, and highly misleading figures are often given. In any event, quantitative comparisons are insufficient because they take no account of geographical advantages, military technology, the ages of military hardware, deployment, training, morale and so on. No one can credibly claim to know what course a conventional war in Europe would take. Still, a dominant perception in Western political and military establishments is that the Warsaw Pact has the upper edge, even though NATO is superior in command, communications and control, electronic-warfare capability, precision-guided munitions and surveillance.

For what it is worth, a 1982 IISS numerical comparison of NATO and Warsaw Pact forces can be summarized as follows: in total ground forces, NATO surpasses the Warsaw Pact 2,125,000 to 1,664,000; the Warsaw Pact is decisively ahead overall in ground force equipment (tanks, artillery, anti-tank and anti-aircraft guns, etc.), and overwhelmingly so if further Soviet divisions were brought in from other fronts; there is rough overall parity with naval units, with NATO leading in surface fleet but not in submarines; NATO is ahead in naval and maritime aircraft but far behind in land-attack aircraft and fighters.

The assumption that the Warsaw Pact would be able to win a conventional European war is now being challenged by many military specialists who know NATO from the inside. In March of 1983, for example, the commander of the U.S. Army in Europe told an interviewer: "It disappoints me to hear people talk about the overwhelming Soviet conventional military strength. We can defend the borders of Western Europe with what we have. I've never asked for a larger force. I do not think that conventional defense is anywhere *near* hopeless."

After a detailed assessment of the current balance of conventional sea, land and air forces, American defense analyst William Kaufman concluded that NATO already has the conventional forces to make a Soviet offensive highly risky. Only after making a series of implausible "worst case" assumptions, he argues, is the standard notion of an overwhelming Warsaw Pact superiority credible.

While the Soviets clearly do have a significant overall conventional superiority in Europe in numerical terms, that superiority is not enough, in itself, to give them a decisive advantage. While it is true that some Soviet weapons have greater range and firepower than NATO artillery, NATO's systems are qualitatively superior and better shielded against enemy fire. And although the Warsaw Pact's total combat airpower seemingly dwarfs NATO's, sixty per cent of the pact's aviation force is made of short-range interceptor aircraft, most of which are suitable only for air defense and not for ground attack.

NATO's combined naval forces are superior to that of the Warsaw Pact both in numbers of surface combatants and in total naval tonnage (a measure of the size of the ships). More importantly, NATO vessels also have direct access to the open ocean. To operate in the European theatre, Soviet Union and Warsaw Pact ships must pass through bottlenecks controlled by NATO and other U.S. allies. In another category, the large tank force of the Warsaw Pact is often cited as a major threat to Western Europe. However, NATO made a decision not to match the Warsaw Pact tank for tank but rather to concentrate on precision-guided anti-tank weapons (the one category of land equipment, according to the IISS estimates, where NATO is clearly ahead).

Another factor, frequently forgotten, is that in combat, all other things being equal, the defense has a decided advantage over the offense. To carry out the kind of blitzkrieg strategy that NATO expects from the Warsaw Pact, the Soviet Union would need a massive military superiority, which it manifestly does not possess. Additionally, the Soviet Union could not count on the reliability of Warsaw Pact armies in the event of war. The old military rule of thumb is that the offense requires a three-to-one advantage over the defense. This is not to suggest that such an advantage would be necessary to ensure victory in Europe, but that an adequate NATO conventional deterrent does not require numerical parity with the Warsaw Pact. A force whose aims are purely defensive does not need to compare the number of its tanks with those of the enemy, or its aircraft with theirs. It is more appropriate for a defensive force to compare its anti-tank forces with enemy tanks and its anti-aircraft defenses with enemy attack aircraft. NATO comes out quite favourably in these less well publicized ratios.

In summary, the argument asserting Warsaw Pact superiority in conventional forces, adduced to justify the need to preserve the concept of NATO's first use of nuclear weapons, is largely groundless. Yet there are no grounds for complacency.

In its 1984-85 report, the IISS notes that NATO has largely lost the technological edge in conventional weapons which had allowed the substitution of quality for numbers. "One cannot necessarily conclude that NATO would suffer defeat in war, nor that the Warsaw Pact would see its advantage as being sufficient to risk an attack," the institute cautions. "But one can conclude that there has been sufficient danger in the trend to require remedies."

The adjustments needed to maintain adequate conventional NATO forces do not require enormous sums of money or the infusion of large quantities of troops. A number of outlines for non-provocative defense systems have been presented, including one by the conservative magazine *The Economist*. The Union of Concerned Scientists suggested in 1983:

> With a number of ready improvements, NATO's margin of safety could be dramatically increased. These improvements include: establishing more efficient allied decision making procedures in times of crisis, improving rapid reinforcement capabilities, constructing simple obstacles and field fortifications in likely corridors of attack, and increasing the availability of pre-positioned supplies.

These changes can be brought about with very small increases in defense spending, particularly if there is a halt in the nuclear weapons build-up going on in Europe. In recent years, advantages in cost and effectiveness have moved decisively from the offensive to the defensive. A study by William Kaufman concludes that the most cost-effective defensive measure would be the construction of an obstacle and fortifications network along the central front, at an estimated cost of less than $1.5 billion. It has been estimated that such a barrier could decrease the effectiveness of an invasion force by as much as forty per cent and greatly reduce the need to use all NATO ground forces in manning the front. This would enable more units to be assigned to mobile reserves and, in Kaufman's view, "reduce to essentially zero the probability that an enemy could achieve even a temporary advance with a smash and grab attack."

Deep Strike

As sensible as this proposal to construct a defensive barrier seems, it has no place in NATO strategy. NATO has chosen a new conventional weapons strategy which is likely to obscure the threshold between conventional and nuclear forces. In what is referred to as a "Follow-On Force Attack," or "deep strike," the intent is to carry the battle back in to Warsaw Pact territory more effectively by using "smart" conventional weapons — guided munitions and conventionally-armed ballistic or Cruise missiles — in order to impede Warsaw Pact forces, destroy Warsaw Pact air bases, and suppress fixed targets such as command and control sites and supply depots. The proponents of deep strike maintain that new conventional-weapons technologies offer a solution to NATO's perceived inferiority in conventional weapons. They claim that deep strike is a comparatively cheap way of raising the nuclear threshold by reducing reliance on nuclear weapons within the NATO doctrine of flexible response.

There are, however, escalatory dangers involved in adopting counter-offensive rather than defensive systems. While NATO has always had a conventional capacity to strike into Eastern Europe, the primary emphasis has been on front-line defense. The capacity for early use of conventional weapons, prior to actual engagement between NATO and Warsaw Pact ground forces, will fundamentally change NATO's posture.

In such a strategy, "anticipation" can trigger miscalculation and the "response" can be delivered by accident. These new, sophisticated non-nuclear weapons will be able to destroy targets on the ground with the effectiveness of small tactical nuclear weapons, further increasing the scope for misunderstanding. All descriptions of deep strike underline the importance of early attack on "time urgent" fixed targets. A parallel development can be expected on the part of the Warsaw Pact and may have already started with the recent forward deployment of Soviet short- and medium-range missiles capable of launching both nuclear and conventional warheads. As this trend continues, more and more targets will become immediately vulnerable on both sides, and the incentive to launch first, in order not to be the one unable to launch at all, grows correspondingly. The implications of this development for stability in a crisis are obvious and ominous. How would the Soviets know that a deep-strike attack was conventional, not nuclear? It may be impossible to distinguish conventionally-armed Cruise missiles from nuclear ones while in flight.

It must also be asked whether the new technology will work. It is extremely difficult to hit accurately a target hundreds of miles away, especially if it is moving. State-of-the-art weapon systems depend on very fragile communications equipment which could be jammed by enemy electronics, confused by bad weather or smoke, or simply destroyed.

Ironically, the style of conventional strategy favoured by NATO will raise rather than lower the risk of nuclear war. The principle that is lacking was supplied by Helmut Schmidt as early as 1962. Schmidt was speaking of his own country, but his rule of thumb applies to all of Western Europe: "The optimum goal of a German defense policy and strategy would ... be the creation of an armament structure clearly unsuited for the offensive role yet adequate beyond the shadow of a doubt to defend German territory." The careful substitution of non-nuclear forces, defensive in character and deployment, can make the escalation of nuclear weapons much less likely. But a provocative build-up of conventional forces tightly integrated with nuclear weapons — especially tactical nuclear weapons subject to a "use them or lose them" dilemma — will only destabilize the peace in Europe.

The Future of European Negotiations

This overview of nuclear and conventional weapons in Europe brings us back full circle to Reagan's "zero option," which in retrospect can be seen as a ploy to secure the deployment, rather than the cancellation, of the Pershing II and Cruise missiles. The Cruise's career as a "bargaining chip" was ended. *If* the U.S. and NATO had needed something to trade away to reduce the Soviets SS-20s, an enlarged complement of Poseidon submarine warheads would have served that purpose without lowering the nuclear threshold.

In fact the logic of a primarily sea-based deterrent had been embraced by Helmut Schmidt, who told the *Washington Post* that "sea-based systems would suit our geographic and strategic conditions better" than the Pershing and Cruise missiles.

An American top-secret State Department document is said to warn that existing submarine-launched ballistic missiles assigned to NATO cannot do the INF job because "they are generally regarded as strategic systems whose use prior to general Nuclear Response might convey an overly escalatory signal to the Soviet Union." But would the Soviet leaders take a first strike with Pershing IIs or ground-launched Cruise missiles any less seriously? As we saw earlier, the fact is that the United States has resisted putting its European "deterrent" out to sea because it would lack — at least at this point in technological development — the precision to be a credible "war-fighting" weapon. The first result of NATO's December 1979 "Two-Track" decision was to delay the start of serious INF negotiations for over two years, during which time the Soviets tripled the SS-20 threat to Western Europe — from 81 to 243.

A balanced European arms limitation agreement would call upon the Russians to dismantle all their SS-4s and SS-5s as well as at least 200 of their SS-20s — this means destroying them, not simply redeploying them behind the Urals — in return for an American agreement to cancel the Pershing II and Cruise deployments. The Soviets have, in fact, indicated that they might find these terms acceptable.

European hopes were revived by the July 1982 "walk in the woods" when chief U.S. INF negotiator Paul Nitze and his Soviet counterpart Yuri Kvitsinsky reportedly reached a tentative agreement. This package, in which the Soviets would have given up their insistence on compensation for British and French nuclear forces, would also have cancelled the Pershing II and substantially reduced the European deployments of both the SS-20 and the Cruise. The agreement would have limited each side to no more than 75 intermediate-range missile launchers. The Soviet Union would have destroyed its 385 older missile launchers — the SS-4s and SS-5s and all but 75 of the SS-20s positioned west of Novosibirsk, a city in southwestern Siberia. Since there were then 243 SS-20s in that huge area, the Soviets would have been committed to destroying 168 of these modern missile launchers. The balance of the Soviet Union's SS-20 force, 90 missile launchers deployed well to the east of Novosibirsk, would have been frozen at that number. The understanding specified that the 75 launchers allowed the Americans could not include any Pershing IIs; these would be banned. But 300 Cruise missiles (4 per launcher) would thus have been permitted.

This proposal, while not without major problems (i.e., Cruise deployment), would have raised the nuclear threshold in Europe. It seemingly had the support of almost all West European governments, but Nitze could get no support in Washington. U.S. Defense Secretary Weinberger referred to the Pershing II as "irreplaceable ... the weapon the Soviets fear most." It would have been fitting to add, "the weapon the U.S. Army wants most." In deciding that the Pershing II was unexpendable, the Reagan administration neglected to consult with the West Europeans. It is interesting that Schmidt and other West German leaders — who were supposedly behind the INF deployment — were particularly disappointed. Willy Brandt, chairman of the

Social Democratic Party and former chancellor, maintained that the potential agreement was vetoed because

> powerful people had taken it into their thick heads that deployment of Pershing II was more important than getting rid of the SS-20s.... In my opinion it happened because the people who guide the U.S. thought they could gain a strategic advantage which corresponds in principle to the one the Soviets tried to institute in Cuba toward the U.S. 20 years ago.

Near the end of 1982 another major Russian proposal was issued, this time by Yuri Andropov, then the general secretary of the Communist Party. He offered to limit the number of Soviet intermediate-range European missiles to the equivalent of the combined nuclear missiles of the United Kingdom and France — 162. The USSR agreed to reduce the number of SS-20 launchers to 120 (360 warheads, reload capabilities not included) and eliminate all remaining SS-4s and SS-5s, in exchange for a promise of no new NATO deployment in Western Europe. That would have brought the number of warheads on Soviet intermediate-range nuclear weapons targeted on Europe below the number that existed before the SS-20 deployments began. Whether these proposals were intended sincerely or merely as ploys in the public contest over the INF issue remains unknown because the U.S. indicated no interest.

The best offer the Americans could counter with was an acknowledgement in early 1983 that the U.S. would accept in principle an "interim agreement" whereby each side would be permitted an equal but reduced number of INF missile warheads. Within three days the Soviet Union rejected the interim approach as a revamped version of the "zero option" which retained U.S. insistence on an equal number of warheads in an American-defined category. The Soviets answered that the interim approach, if accepted, would result in Soviet reductions simultaneously with new American deployments. Indeed, the behaviour of the Reagan administration raised serious and widespread doubts whether there ever was any American intention to reach a reasonable agreement. As Lawrence Freedman, an unusually candid establishment voice, has remarked:

> Those responsible for the [NATO "two-track"] program hoped from the start that the addition of an arms-control offer to the force-modernization plans would be sufficient to deflect the opposition. It was never envisaged that arms control would lead to the abandonment of the plans for 572 Cruise and Pershing missiles, but sufficient slack was built into the numbers to allow for substantial reductions in the name of arms control.

The Legacy of the Cruise and Pershing II

The deployment of Cruise and Pershing II missiles has meant forfeiting all hope of an INF agreement at relatively low levels. It may also quadruple the SS-20 threat of late 1979. McGeorge Bundy argues that NATO modernization is a pyrrhic victory:

> It is not self-evident, to put it very gently, that the "victory" of December 1983, and the safe arrival in Europe of the first ground-launched Cruise missiles and Pershing IIs, has left the Alliance stronger and more self-confident than it would have been if it had been decided in 1977 and thereafter that there was nothing in any new Soviet deployment of any sort that

required a change in the decision of the 1960s that the right place for American mid-range nuclear weapons supporting NATO was in submarines at sea.

As a consequence of the NATO deployments, Moscow has announced its intention to put the U.S. in an "analogous position" through a series of countermeasures — some of which may be little more than a repackaging of existing Soviet programs. An unspecified number of shorter-range (under 620 miles) SS-22 missiles are being deployed in East Germany and in Czechoslovakia, manned by Soviet troops. New SS-23 missiles are likely to follow. The moratorium on the deployment of SS-20s within striking range of Europe has been lifted. In explicit response to the short flight time of the Pershing II, the USSR is reported to be deploying submarine-launched ballistic missiles nearer than before to the U.S. coastline. Russia has already begun flight tests of an updated, more accurate version of the SS-20.

The overall import of Pershing II and Cruise deployment, made in the name of greater security, is a dramatic lowering of the European nuclear threshold. The members of Generals for Peace conclude: "As the reality of the situation impresses itself on people, the realization will follow that we are safer without these weapons than with them."

5
Canada as a Nuclear Innocent

C.D. Howe, Ottawa's pre-eminent power broker in the postwar era, reacted to the bombing of Hiroshima by releasing a statement that admitted it was "a particular pleasure to announce that Canadian scientists have played an intimate part, and have been associated in an effective way, with this great scientific development."

Howe's comment notwithstanding, Canada after the war appeared to offer a shining example to the rest of the world. In 1945, this country could have developed its own nuclear bomb readily. Canada chose not to and, at least in this respect, offered a model for non-proliferation.

During John Diefenbaker's time in power, Canada temporarily lost its image of nuclear innocence by agreeing to acquire four nuclear weapon systems. Two — the Bomarc anti-aircraft missile and the Genie nuclear-tipped missile carried by the CF-101 Voodoo — were to be used to defend North America from Soviet air attack. The other two — the Honest John short-range nuclear missile and the nuclear-armed CF-104 — were to be used in NATO roles in Europe. Reversing his anti-nuclear campaign plank, Lester Pearson gave the go-ahead for these nuclear weapons after his election victory in 1963. Pierre Trudeau opposed the nuclear policy of Pearson, calling him "the defrocked priest of peace," and began to change it immediately upon becoming prime minister a few years later. In 1969 Canada stripped its forces in Europe of nuclear weapons. Honest John nuclear missiles were taken away from Canada's ground forces in Europe and CF-104 Starfighters based at Lahr, West Germany, were given a ground support and reconnaissance role, using conventional weapons. Canada's air roles in NATO were altered from nuclear bombing to reconnaissance and conventional ground support. Within North American aerospace defense, the Bomarc was retired in 1971. When the Voodoo interceptor was replaced in November of 1984 by the CF-18 Hornet, conventional rockets replaced nuclear missiles as the air-defense weapon. Canada's Conservative government stated categorically in 1985 that nuclear weapons will not be allowed on our soil in peacetime.

Canadians may take this country's nuclear celibacy for granted, but the United States apparently does not. William Arkin, a military analyst with the Washington-based Institute for Policy Studies, disclosed in 1984 that in periods when U.S. forces are in a state of "advanced readiness," the Pentagon intends to move nuclear depth charges to Canadian maritime bases at Comox, British Columbia and Greenwood, Nova Scotia for use in anti-submarine warfare. The plans are part of an annual classified memo signed by President Reagan that authorizes all deployment of American nuclear weapons outside the U.S. Robert Falls, retired admiral and former chief of Canada's defense staff, declared that "The United States has a moral obligation to consult us when using our territory for something as emotional as nuclear weapons. It is an immoral attitude to make plans without consulting the countries involved." Falls also revealed that U.S. nuclear deployment plans had never been discussed in the councils of NATO: "The implication is they're saying 'To hell with you little guys, Icelanders, Bermudans, Canadians, we're going to do it anyway!'" External Affairs Minister Joe Clark maintained that "this government would be prepared to exercise our option to refuse ... if we believed that to be in the interests of Canada." But Clark's assurances did little to quiet opposition claims that Canada would be powerless to stop the U.S. from stationing nuclear weapons here if Americans felt it was in *their* interest.

A few months later (March 1985) Arkin and an associate, Richard Fieldhouse, used the U.S. Freedom of Information Act to obtain information revealing that U.S. bombers loaded with nuclear bombs, nuclear short-range attack missiles and air-launched Cruise missiles would disperse to Cold Lake and other Canadian air fields during a crisis. While American plans are to deploy nuclear depth charges in Canada only in the event of an actual war scare, the B-52 alert procedures provide for dispersal "in the face of increasing enemy threat or heightened international tensions." The Americans appear to have given themselves some latitude here. During the 1962 Cuban missile crisis U.S. bomber squadrons scattered to U.S. civilian air fields. Canadian fields might well expect a similar visitation in the future. Canada does prohibit the storage of American nuclear weapons on its soil. But because the nuclear weapons on board U.S. planes would stay inside the aircraft, and thus technically would not be on Canadian soil, the U.S. military considers that Canadian policy would not be violated. This is a subtle difference indeed.

The American attitude is not actually that presumptuous. Despite its non-nuclear halo, Canada has been a willing auxiliary to American nuclear weapons policy since the development of the Hiroshima and Nagasaki bombs. As Ernie Regehr of Project Ploughshares has put it, Canada has had "about as intimate an involvement as is possible without actually becoming defined as a nuclear weapons state."

Canada does not "own" nuclear weapons, but Canada does help to develop and build them. The testing of the Cruise missile and the production of its guidance system are the most visible examples. Canadian companies make parts for American Trident nuclear submarines and the cranes used to arm the subs with warheads. They have also made launchers for the neutron bomb delivery system and Alberta has been used as a proving ground for neutron bomb artillery shells.

It is in the area of nuclear infrastructure that Canada most actively connects with nuclear war-fighting developments, including the increasing militarization of space. As a country with non-nuclear policies, it is ironic that Canada is second only to West Germany in the number (nearly eighty) of nuclear weapons-related facilities on its soil. For example:

- Canada takes part in research on how satellite communications are transmitted in northern latitudes. This includes studying high-frequency communications between Canadian Forces Station (CFS) Alert on Ellesmere Island and two American experimental satellites. CFS Alert, the northernmost active military installation to which the U.S. has access, also serves in research on the new Milstar satellite, the premier U.S. system for communication in what the U.S. military calls a "potential war."

Canada as a Nuclear Innocent 145

- Both the Canadian Armed Forces and the Canadian defense industry are cooperating in the development of the Navstar Global Positioning System of eighteen satellites which are to beam radio signals to earth receivers for precise navigational information. While the system, to be operational by the end of this decade, has compelling civilian applications, its more disturbing function will be to enhance the accuracy of sea-based ballistic missiles, giving them first-strike capabilities. The Canadian forces have two officers in key positions in the Navstar project, and the Canadian Marconi Corporation is producing the Navstar user terminal and receiver. According to former Minister of National Defense Jean-Jacques Blais, the defense department has provided over $6 million in development funding, and procurement funding will exceed $50 million.
- Many secret communications programs are being developed for operation in Canada. The Ground Wave Emergency Network (GWEN), for example, which the United States began to deploy in 1983, is scheduled to extend into Canada. It will connect Canadian air bases with U.S. command centres as a "surviving" communications system after a nuclear exchange between the U.S. and the USSR.
- The U.S. Navy uses the Advanced Underwater Acoustic Measurement System at Jervis Inlet and the Maritime Experimental and Test Range at Nanoose Bay, both in British Columbia, as testing and training areas for anti-submarine weapons (ASW). Canadian Aurora maritime patrol aircraft serve American ASW operations centres throughout the world by supplying targeting data on Soviet submarines. This participation is significant because the development of U.S. systems for finding and

attacking Soviet submarines could destabilize the nuclear balance. If the Soviets became convinced that important elements in their nuclear submarine fleet were threatened, they might, in a crisis, be tempted to launch their submarine missiles in a first strike rather than see them destroyed. (U.S. strategic submarines would remain relatively safe because of the comparable freedom they enjoy to travel the world's oceans.)
- The Baker-Nunn satellite tracking camera at St. Margarets, New Brunswick is part of the U.S. Air Force Spacetrack system which will be used to target anti-satellite weapons and which contributes to the development of anti-satellite weapons.
- NORAD is at the heart of a program to integrate communications and command systems for the U.S. Strategic Defense Initiative.

As the above list suggests, a characteristic Canadian role in weapons research and development has been to provide test space for both nuclear and conventional systems. This policy is a natural result of the resource Canada has in abundance: open space. From 1959 to 1972, Canada helped the U.S. in the joint turbulent hypersonic weight program, studying phenomena associated with a space capsule's or a missile's re-entry into the earth's atmosphere. Between 1966 and 1970, the Canadian forces undertook evaluation of Abbot howitzers for the British. Between 1978 and 1983, Canada helped the U.S. in variable depth sonar trials in Nanoose, British Columbia. The list goes on. In fact, in fiscal year 1983-84, the rental of training and testing facilities to foreign governments amounted to 51.8 per cent of the Department of National Defense's revenue of $324 million. In 1977, a senior engineer at the Nanoose torpedo test range offered this explanation of his role, which could stand as an epitaph to Canada's part in the preparation for World War III: "We are told what is to be tested, we do it and report back what we find. We don't even comment on efficiency or suggested modifications."

Building the Cruise's Brain

The best known economic link between Canada and the nuclear arms race is Litton Systems (Canada) Ltd. of Rexdale, Ontario, which describes itself as the "world's leading producer of inertial navigation systems for military aircraft" and builds elements of the Cruise missile's electronic guidance system. Like most defense manufacturers in Canada, Litton is a branch plant of an American multinational. Through its Defense Industry Productivity Programme (DIPP), the federal government has given Litton a grant of $26.4 million to subsidize production of the Cruise guidance system. For the same purpose, the government has given the company a five-year, interest-free loan of $22.5 million.

(DIPP is designed to enhance Canada's industrial base. Grants are made for research and development, to help establish a Canadian company as a qualified supplier of defense or defense-related products, to support related modernization projects, and for market feasibility studies. In 1977, the government spent $43 million on DIPP; by 1983 the figure had soared to $169.2 million. DIPP grants now represent almost 20 cents on every dollar of Canadian military export to the U.S.)

The first Litton delivery of a $200,000 Cruise unit was made on April 10, 1981 to the U.S. Joint (Air

Force-Navy) Cruise Missile Project. Litton had two contracts from the U.S. Defense Department for 102 guidance systems in fiscal year 1981-82 and 305 in 1982-83. The contracts were worth $80 million to Litton. But in 1984 the company failed to get the Pentagon contract to produce the guidance system for the U.S. advanced Cruise missile. The president of Litton blamed Canadian "peace protesters" in a message to his employees: "They are an irritant, they got a lot of publicity ... and the Americans read every damn piece of it." The coveted contract went to the Kearfott Division of the Singer Co. in Little Falls, New Jersey. In fact, Litton's loss of the contract probably had nothing to do with protests in Canada; there had been considerable dissatisfaction with Litton in the Pentagon.

The manufacturing of components for the Cruise missile and other American nuclear weapon systems in Canada is grounded in the 1959 Defense Production Sharing Arrangement (DPSA) — a kind of Auto Pact of the weapons industry. The agreement formalized a "rough balance" of arms trade between the two countries. For Canadian firms this means producing parts for weapon systems designed and developed in the U.S. The economic benefits derived from such activity — whether for the Cruise, other weapons or potential SDI projects — are often cited by industry spokesmen. But for the Canadian government this "balance" means that for every dollar of military parts exported to the U.S., the Department of National Defense (DND) must import one dollar of completed American weapons. Thus there is no benefit in terms of balance of trade. In fact, the DPSA is a source of foreign-exchange loss for the Canadian economy. Between 1971 and 1984 Canada spent $1.6 billion more than it earned through the DPSA program. This situation is complicated by the fact that in much of its sub-contract work for U.S. weapon systems, Canadian industry is building to U.S. design specifications. This means that many of the tools and supplies required must be imported from the U.S. According to a Statistics Canada analysis, for every dollar of military commodities exported to the U.S., Canada must first import twenty cents worth of machine tools and other equipment. As economist Mel Watkins concludes, "there is no net benefit to the Canadian economy and no net increase in jobs.... For economic reasons alone, we ought to cancel the DPSA."

The DPSA has helped to produce a severely truncated industry in Canada — a classic branch-plant industry. The Canadian military, with very few exceptions, can carry out only specific, limited functions within the broad range of activities normally identified with national defense. And Canada's military industry performs only specialized, regional tasks within an integrated continental industry. It is dependent on a single market — the United States. For the majority of Canadian-produced military commodities there is no domestic market, not because Canada does not buy enough completed equipment, but because Canada buys from American suppliers.

Cruise Testing

The Canadian management of the American request to test the Cruise provides an interesting study in how Ottawa decides defense issues. The question was reduced to one of how to minimize public relations damage; whether it was right or necessary for Canada to test the Cruise was never faced head on.

American interest in testing several new weapons systems in Canada first came to the attention of the Canadian Defense Liaison staff in Washington in June of 1978. In August of 1978, research and development officials of the two defense departments began to consider expanding cooperation to include the testing of an electro-optical guided weapon such as the Cruise missile in an unrestricted environment "which Canada's geography and climate could provide better than that of the U.S." Testing arrangements were subsequently discussed during a number of meetings of the Canada-U.S. Permanent Joint Board on Defense. The Strategic Air Command of the U.S. Air Force presented the Canadian DND with the first Cruise testing proposal in late 1979.

The Canadian public's first inkling of Canada's direct involvement with the Cruise missile came in October of 1980 when Dr. William Perry, the Pentagon's senior scientist, hinted to the press that Canada could be helpful by providing space for testing the Cruise. According to U.S. Air Force officials, "the terrain and climatic conditions in Northern Canada would offer a good opportunity to test the inertial guidance system of the Cruise missile under conditions similar to those in the Soviet Union." Shortly thereafter, the Carter administration presented a formal proposal to the Canadian government.

Aware of the potential for a "political storm" over the request, officials in the DND developed a two-step strategy to ensure acceptance of the American proposal. Although the U.S. originally requested a single "umbrella" agreement, the DND asked the Pentagon to first agree on a framework accord, entitled the Canada-United States Test and Evaluation Program (CANUSTEP), with the understanding that this document, because it was not linked to any specific weapon and hence was likely to be received less vociferously by the peace movement, would defuse opposition to a subsequent Cruise testing agreement. The CANUSTEP agreement, if kept quiet, would allow the DND more time to influence public opinion and secure Cabinet approval.

At a meeting in Ottawa on April 15, 1981, U.S. Defense Secretary Caspar Weinberger presented the Reagan administration's Cruise proposal to Canadian Minister of National Defense Gilles Lamontagne. During July of 1981, the proposal was discussed in the Cabinet Committee on Foreign and Defense Policy, and during October and November, in the Cabinet Committee on Priorities and Planning.

The first news of the government's commitment reached the Canadian public after March 10, 1982, when a U.S. Air Force official in the Pentagon leaked the information to a Canadian journalist. The Canadian government's plans to "keep a lid on" the issue were scuttled. When questioned in the House of Commons, the secretary of state for external affairs, Mark MacGuigan, acknowledged that a framework agreement had been discussed with the United States. Although many of his colleagues, including the prime minister, continued to deny the existence of any such agreement, an internal government memorandum subsequently proved that

> the Canadian agreement in principle permitting the Secretary of State for External Affairs to negotiate and conclude a bilateral agreement on the matter was transmitted to the United States during December 1981 in a letter from Prime Minister Trudeau to President Reagan in response to a letter from the President supporting the proposal.

At an Ottawa dinner for U.S. Vice-President George Bush, some guests say they heard Prime Minister Trudeau remark, "Don't worry George, we'll test the Cruise for you."

In February of 1983, Canada signed the five-year CANUSTEP agreement, allowing the defense departments of the two countries to arrange specific testing projects. According to the Department of External Affairs, the "systems to be tested under the agreement could include artillery equipment, helicopters, surveillance and identification systems, advanced non-nuclear munitions, aircraft navigation systems, and the guidance system for unarmed Cruise missiles."

The deal was made. Without any prior debate in Parliament, the Liberals tied Canadians to projects they may never hear about. As Prime Minister Trudeau admitted on a CBC radio talk show, the decision was taken with "no direct consultation with anyone in Canada." Either the U.S. or Canada can request that actual details be kept secret, so it is impossible to know the extent and range of Canada's obligations. The agreement could even involve Canada in the development of weapons that could be used in countries with which Canada has friendly relations.

On June 13, 1983, The U.S. went on to formally request that Canada permit operational testing of the ALCM at the Primrose Lake test range in Alberta. On July 15, 1983, having taken the maximum time to respond to the American request, Minister of External Affairs Allan MacEachen and Minister of Defense Gilles Lamontagne annnounced that the ALCM would be tested in Canada during the winter months over the following five years. The decision was justified as Canada's contribution to the security of NATO and the West. MacEachen explained that Canada's Cruise policy was based on "several elements": Canada's founding membership in NATO, the government's dedication to global peace and arms control, and Canada's "longstanding decision not to develop our own nuclear force."

In spite of enormous public opposition, the first Canadian Cruise test took place March 6, 1984; a B-52 carrying four missiles slung under its wings flew low, in what is called a "captive-carry mode," over the Canadian Forces Base in Cold Lake, Alberta. Three more tests were held before 1985 was out, two of them free-flight launches testing the guidance system. By the end of 1985 Washington had made six new requests under the umbrella weapons-testing pact. Contrary to expectations, the "stealth" version of the Cruise being developed by General Dynamics was not among the six. But Cruise tests planned for 1986 are expected to include a Star Wars-related experiment (see Chapter 7).

Economic Retaliation

The primary reason invoked for agreeing to test the Cruise — that is, to be a good alliance member — has some rather large holes in it, to which we'll return. There is good reason to believe that the actual key criterion in the Canadian government's deliberations was the American response. Would the U.S. respond to a "no" with economic retaliation, either in the defense industry, or in another disputatious sector? Canadian decision-makers are largely governed by what University of Toronto professor Abraham Rotstein calls the "law of anticipated reactions vis-à-vis the United States." Decisions by Canadian leaders generally take account of American interests in order to avoid conflicts and invite benefits. According to a senior policy advisor in the Prime Minister's Office, "Trudeau considered the testing agreements to be indirectly linked to a number of implied American commitments." A briefing note from Ross Francis of External Affairs Defense Relations to minister Mark MacGuigan suggested the possibility of U.S. economic sanctions if Canada refused to test the Cruise: "While it is difficult to indicate with any degree of specificity what the [U.S.] Administration would do, there is no doubt that its disappointment would colour the relationship [with Canada] in all its facets, including trade and economic."

In September of 1982, U.S. Defense Secretary Caspar Weinberger intervened personally to quash a measure introduced into the U.S. House of Representatives that would have limited the importation of specialty minerals to the United States. This bill would have disqualified millions of dollars worth of defense exports from Canada to the U.S. The administration's support of Canada's lobbying efforts to prevent the measure did not go unnoticed in Ottawa, which also realized that Weinberger could lose heart if Ottawa decided to be uncooperative about Cruise-missile testing.

U.S. Vice-President Bush refused to speculate on the consequences of a Canadian refusal: "I learned long ago not to go into what would happen if a frog had wings." But, in the DPSA, the U.S. has the perfect tool for economic retaliation. It is here that the two aspects of Canada's participation in American nuclear systems — infrastructure and auxiliary functions (like Cruise testing) and manufacturing (as with the Cruise guidance system) — meet, and reinforce each other. There is essentially no alternative market (in Canada or overseas) for the components produced by the Canadian military industry, and the U.S. market for these parts has in recent years been expanding rapidly — from approximately $400 million annually to an estimated $1 billion. If that market were to dry up, damage would be done to the Canadian aerospace and electronics industries.

Addressing the prospect of lost jobs, Robert White, director of the United Auto Workers Canada, remarked: "We must make a decision whether the escalation of the arms race is more important than job security." But moral considerations do not even need to be brought into play in questioning the need to avoid retaliation at all costs. Economic reasons are sufficient. To begin with, the fear of economic repercussions is overblown. Under the DPSA, Canada is required to maintain a rough balance between exports and imports of arms. If Washington pushes Ottawa by lowering Canada's exports, then Canada will be obliged to purchase fewer weapons from the U.S. The net effect is zero whether the U.S. cancels the DPSA or not. Furthermore, on strictly economic terms, the defense industry deserves less support than many other sectors. Because it is highly capital intensive, the defense industry is a particularly poor producer of jobs relative to other areas of the economy. This point was made by Thomas Maxwell, chief economist of the Conference Board of Canada, to military and industry personnel at a 1984 meeting of the Canadian Institute of Strategic Studies:

> If you are looking for an increase in defense expenditure for its macro-economic impact on the economy, then everybody else can play the same game, and some can play it better than you can — they have a better claim in terms of getting the unemployment rate down. So you will have to look for different reasons.

In 1967, Prime Minister Pearson claimed that a major benefit of the DPSA was the large contribution this agreement had made and was continuing to make to Canadian industrial research and development and thus to Canadian high technology. In fact, recent studies by the Science Council of Canada have shown the opposite to be the case. Reports on multinational corporations and innovation in Canadian industry show that the links between Canadian and American industry lead to the transfer of research and development activities to the U.S., and to increased Canadian reliance on production licences from the U.S. Canadian manufacturers end up with what are mostly short-run tasks performed according to Pentagon specifications. As Ernie Regehr points out, "this tends to preclude indigenous design and development of commodities that can ultimately go into mass production and then compete on the basis of lower per unit production costs in an international market." Opportunities for sales abroad just don't arise. For an international corporation, this pattern of control can be profitable; for the host nation, it can have disastrous consequences in the long run.

Military research and development are seldom applicable to other industrial sectors. As long as financing and guarantees are provided by the government and ensure high profit returns for the production of military equipment, there is little incentive for a corporation to consider the costly research and development required to adapt a product for the civilian market. This is why a number of American economists have concluded that the defense industry undermines rather than enhances civilian technology. In Canada the technology transferred from American military contractors usually bears security and economic restrictions prohibiting its conversion to alternative applications. In this way the technology can be regulated to benefit only the parent corporation or the economy of the nation where the technology was developed.

If the Canadian government were to dismantle DPSA and cancel DIPP, it could in the place of these agreements provide funds for conversion programs and help set up research facilities for civilian products. For example, Litton Systems could turn its sonar, sensor and radar technology toward the manufacture of sight aids for the blind and of automatic accident-avoidance systems for cars and aircraft.

It is true that the U.S. could respond very broadly to such Canadian actions. Many Canadian products could be denied access to the U.S. market, and the high level of integration between the two economies makes Canada very vulnerable to such a course of action. Yet Washington would have to consider the fact that this economic intertwining cuts both ways: Canada is the most important trading partner of the U.S., buying twice as much as the next most important partner, Japan. The U.S. cannot move against Canada in the economic sphere without harming some American interests and/or poisoning the overall relationship.

As for Canada, it is well documented that the dependency on resource exports to the U.S. and on branch plant manufacturing is not particularly beneficial to this country even in the best of times. The federal government would be well advised to rearrange Canada's industrial activity in such a way that Canada can decide defense policy questions, such as Cruise testing, on their own merits and not in response to economic threats. One fact stands out clearly: the more Canadian industry becomes a cog in the U.S. military machine, the less flexibility Canada will have to pursue an out-of-step foreign policy.

Canada's NATO "Obligations"

Probably the biggest red herring in the Cruise debate is Canada's supposed NATO obligation to test the missile. Pierre Trudeau declared that Canada would be "a pretty poor partner of the alliance" if it did not agree to the American request. But it is wrong to imply, as Trudeau did, that Canadians have to choose between pulling out of the Western defense organization and allowing American Cruise missiles to be tested here. William Epstein, a Canadian who is past director of disarmament at the United Nations, puts the question squarely: "Does loyalty to NATO and to its leading member require the blind acceptance of or silent acquiescence in every direction and decision of the United States? Surely not, especially when those decisions or actions can put in jeopardy the very survival of our society and civilization." NATO membership is not predicated on accepting increasing nuclear roles. At present, fully ten of the fifteen countries that make up the North Atlantic Treaty Organization have no nuclear weapons of their own. These include such nations as Denmark, Norway, Greece and Iceland. Nor do they want to join the nuclear club. Norway refused to test the Cruise; not only will Denmark not accept the Cruise missiles on its soil, but its parliament voted to refuse payment of its share of the cost of placing them on German soil. So it is incorrect to suggest that Canada would not be a fit NATO partner if it refused the Cruise. While it is true that NATO has a general agreement dating back to 1979 to upgrade its nuclear forces in Europe, the agreement does not require Canada

— or any other member country, for that matter — to get closely involved in the process.

The Cruise testing is not a NATO request at all but comes to Canada under the provision of a bilateral agreement (CANUSTEP). Furthermore, the air-launched version of the Cruise missile, which is a strategic weapon, is entirely independent of NATO forces. The ground-launched Cruise missiles being deployed in Europe have already been tested over terrain similar to that which they would encounter on a flight path from Britain, Central Europe or Sicily to points in the Soviet Union.

While the strategic and economic reasons for testing the Cruise are elusive, a price still has to be paid for them. Testing the Cruise missile has further integrated Canada with U.S. defense planning and has introduced Canada to a far more active role on the nuclear-weapons stage. Testing has also restricted Canada's manoeuvring room as a third party that could help prod the superpowers toward arms reduction. As George Woodcock has written: "So far as Canada is concerned, to allow the testing of the Cruise here will mean our identification in the eyes of the world with the most belligerent of U.S. policies." The minority report submitted by an all-party group of six MPs to the Standing Committee on External Affairs and National Defense agreed: "By allowing tests of new nuclear weapons delivery vehicles such as the Cruise missile which is attack-oriented, Canada risks its credibility as a voice for peace."

Unilateral Disarmament vs. a Freeze

In addition to the "good alliance member" argument, Trudeau, and other backers of Cruise testing, also maintained that to refuse the U.S. would amount to unilateral disarmament. But as earlier chapters have shown, the West already has a mighty nuclear deterrent. The Pentagon does not need the 10,000 Cruise missiles it is planning to add to its arsenal; in any event they can hardly be "disarmed" before they exist!

Refusing to test the Cruise missile would not have constituted unilateral disarmament. Canada would simply have been refusing to go ahead with *more* armaments. After all, there was never any protest about unilateral disarmament when President Carter declined to introduce the B-1 bomber or the neutron bomb. William Epstein has pointed out that there has been a failure to differentiate between sensible restraint and unilateral disarmament: "It is sensible restraint when a country decides not to take an action or not to develop a new weapon which would be against its interests."

What undermines the legitimacy of complaining about unilateral disarmament is that Canada has not lent its support to proposals for bilateral disarmament. The Trudeau government consistently opposed the nuclear-freeze initiative, which would halt the development, production, testing and deployment of all nuclear weapon systems. The Trudeau government questioned the verifiability of a freeze, but turned around and agreed to test the Cruise missile which, especially when deployed at sea, is the weapon system which will most complicate the verifiability of future arms limitation agreements. As Doug Roche argued (before he was appointed Canadian ambassador for disarmament): "If you are for a freeze, then you are against Cruise testing."

Unfortunately, the Conservative government has continued the Canadian tradition of being among only a dozen nations opposed to a freeze. External Affairs Minister Joe Clark has used the old argument that

Canada cannot afford to violate the solidarity of NATO. Six NATO members — Denmark, Greece, Holland, Norway, Spain and Iceland — have not gone along with this point of view. The Conservative government has also suggested that a freeze would be harmful because it would lock in that great bugbear, Soviet superiority.

One final myth employed in favour of Cruise testing needs to be laid to rest. Pierre Trudeau argued in his open letter defending testing that "the anti-Americanism of some Canadians verges on hypocrisy." From Trudeau's definition it might be inferred that the U.S. Catholic bishops and the majority in the House of Representatives, groups that have backed a nuclear freeze, are also "anti-American." Gene LaRocque, now director of the U.S. Centre for Defense Information, has urged Canada not to be an accomplice in Washington's rearmament drive: "It is wrong to test the Cruise missile in Canada. It is wrong to build the Cruise missile. Canadians should stand up and decide what is right for themselves and not always do what the U.S. wants."

6
Can Star Wars Work?

On March 23, 1983, President Ronald Reagan startled the world with his famous "Star Wars" speech in which he promised that the U.S. would combine radically new technologies in a way that would render "nuclear weapons impotent and obsolete." There is little doubt that at the time of the speech, Reagan had no substantial technical analysis to support his position on the feasibility of strategic defense against ballistic missiles. Those in the U.S. government responsible for such matters were unaware of the president's position until the day of the speech. To paraphrase Lewis Carroll, it was a case of "first the sentence, then the trial."

When Reagan announced his Strategic Defense Initiative (SDI), as "Star Wars" is formally known, only a few people on the fringes of nuclear policymaking believed it viable: retired General Daniel Graham and physicist Edward Teller, to name two. The technologies involved had only recently escaped the realm of science fiction. Yet by 1984 SDI was the centrepiece of the Pentagon's nuclear strategy and was dominating national security debates. In April of 1984, Secretary of Defense Caspar Weinberger announced the appointment of Lt. Gen. James A. Abrahamson as head of the newly formed Strategic Defense Initiative Program Office. The Pentagon was looking to spend enormous sums of money on SDI. Administration estimates put the cost of the first five years of Star Wars research at $26 billion. After investing $1.4 billion in 1985, the Pentagon is seeking $3.7 billion for 1986. Congress, however, has tentatively cut the president's 1986 SDI budget down to $2.75 billion. Nonetheless, the administration is still shooting for $21 billion in Star Wars funding over the next five years. John Pike of the Federation of American Scientists pegs the bill for development of Star Wars weapons at more than $90 billion by 1994 and costs may eventually far exceed $500 billion.

The thought of a perfect defense against missiles is immensely attractive. Would it not be virtually ideal if we could actually construct a defensive shield to prevent the ravages of nuclear war? But there are formidable obstacles to re-creating the world that disappeared when the nuclear bomb was born. For one, Star Wars may not be technologically feasible. It may also violate existing arms control agreements with the Soviet Union. But above all, it may be strategically undesirable. The attempt to install space defenses could precipitate a nuclear conflict that would not be confined to space.

The major issues in strategic defense will be addressed from two areas of concern. This chapter will deal with the question of whether SDI is technically feasible. Chapter 7 will focus on explicitly strategic issues: is a defense against missiles strategically desirable? Does it enhance or diminish stability and the prospects for arms control and nuclear disarmament? Chapter 7 will also look at Canada's role in SDI and the uses being planned for this new technology should a perfect defense prove unattainable.

The Pursuit of Perfect Technology

The dramatic expansion of the ability to gather, process and transmit vast quantities of data efficiently has made it possible to get high quality intelligence from distant parts of the earth and space. The properties of attacks can now be discriminated and assessed very promptly.

Concurrently, great strides have been made in the ability to produce, focus and aim laser and particle beams of increasingly high power. These new "bullets" of directed energy travel at or near the velocity of light and, along with "kinetic" weapons that use magnetic energy to fire projectiles, have led to revolutionary ideas for defense against ballistic missiles. Such advances in the science of managing a defense and quickly attacking distant targets have eliminated a number of shortcomings in previous defense concepts.

One salient technical fact has not changed with time: the power of nuclear weapons is overwhelmingly destructive. Rendering nuclear weapons "impotent and obsolete" still requires a defense that is almost perfect — for if only a fraction of the Soviet arsenal gets through the shield, many parts of North America would still be devastated. Technical assessments of SDI concepts cannot escape this awesome requirement.

Certainly there are serious technical problems with SDI. Some have to do with the nature of the beams. For example, because laser beams tend to spread out as they propagate, it would be difficult to concentrate enough energy in a beam to rapidly disable a missile at a range of approximately 600 miles. Charged particle beams can be deflected and distorted by the earth's magnetic field, rendering them useless. Other problems arise from the demands placed on the hardware. The phrase "defensive technologies" may conjure up images of mighty fortifications, but in the case of SDI it refers to delicate instruments: huge mirrors of exquisite precision, ultra-sensitive detectors of heat and radiation, optical systems that must find a one-foot target that is thousands of miles away and moving at four miles per second. All these marvels must work near the theoretical verge of perfection; even small losses in precision would lead to unacceptably poor performance. Quite feeble blows by anti-satellite weapons against orbiting "battle stations" bearing such crown jewels of technology could render the instruments worthless.

A system of defense against ballistic missiles requires many components, all of which are crucial to its effective operation. A first set of space-based sensors provides early warning of an attack. Communication links relay the warning to analysis centres, to the command centres which make decisions as to the appropriate national response, and to the military forces themselves. A second set of sensors acquires, discriminates and tracks targets; points and fires; and later assesses the attack. Finally there are the interceptors of directed energy sources (i.e., lasers and particle beams) that make the kill. There are three phases in a ballistic missile's trajectory where attack might be possible: the "boost phase," mid-course and terminal phase. It is the boost phase that is critical to SDI planners. After launch, the "bus" laden with individually targeted warheads is hoisted through the atmosphere and into space by rockets (which burn out and fall away). There would be an obvious advantage in timing defensive attacks during the boost phase: all the warheads carried on a single rocket could be destroyed by a single attack. Moreover, in the boost phase the flaming rocket emits an intense infra-red signal that can greatly facilitate detection. But there are formidable — and perhaps insoluble — technical problems in destroying rockets during this first phase.

An effective defense would have to be close to the missiles. It would have to be able to attack about 2,000 Soviet boosters within three to five minutes after they emerge from their silos or submarine hatches — before they move outside the atmosphere and release their independently targeted warheads. Physicist Richard Garwin, a long-time defense consultant to the Pentagon and a Star Wars critic, jokingly suggests that the surest defense would be to station American machine gunners a few yards from the Soviet silos and let them strafe the boosters as they lift off. Barring that, the U.S. must find a way to attack the boosters quickly from long range, a prospect Garwin finds nearly as unlikely as the Soviets allowing enemy machine gunners near their missile silos. The problem of "booster-busting" has affected the relative prominence of laser, particle beam and kinetic weapons in SDI forecasting.

Because of the need for lightning speed, the earliest planning for SDI favoured laser beams, which move at the speed of light, to do the booster-busting. Of the three types of lasers under consideration by the Pentagon, the prime contender is a chemical laser, which creates a high-intensity infra-red beam and burns hydrogen and fluorine as fuels. (The other two types are excimer and X-ray lasers.) Since a laser beam must dwell on a target long enough to burn a hole in it or melt its internal mechanism, it requires enormous quantities of energy and fuel to operate. If based on the ground, its beam power would be dissipated in passing through the atmosphere long before it reached a missile. The use of laser weapons would require approximately 300 1,000-megawatt power plants. One arms expert has said waggishly: "The Pentagon's got a better idea — a long extension cord."

Once a favourite, the particle beam weapon is a device that uses the technology of particle accelerators to direct a beam of electrically charged particles (such as neutrons) at a target. Researchers at Los Alamos National Laboratory in New Mexico have proved that such devices can create a barrage of neutrons strong enough to smash through the shell of a missile, but so far, they have measured the effective distance in yards.

Recently, kinetic weapons have gained favour over the laser and the particle-beam weapons within the U.S. administration. One such weapon, the railgun, accelerates chunks of ammunition called "smart rocks." But kinetic weapons are limited in range to about 930 miles, and to station enough of them in space to counter the Soviet missile arsenal would require orbiting about 500 satellites, each carrying about 100 of the guns. The highest velocity now attainable by railguns is about 5.3 miles per second. This is much too slow to intercept boosters. For railgun projectiles to operate at higher speeds, they would require active cooling, although this could be achieved by boosting off fluid stored inside. Kinetic weapons also require a remarkably precise aiming mechanism, given that the projectiles they fire are much too small to contain any kind of homing device.

In order to put these weapons near enough to Soviet silos or nuclear submarines, one proposal is to build and launch into space a large fleet of battle stations (each weighing approximately 100 tons). If orbiting the earth in sufficient numbers, there would be enough of them over a launching area at any moment to attack Soviet rockets with lasers or particle beams. The stations could be placed either in low orbits just outside the atmosphere (about 620 miles) or in geo-stationary orbits some 21,800 miles out. In the latter case the stations would only appear to be stationary. Their orbit would be exactly in step with the earth's. Either option presents formidable difficulties.

Stations with low orbits would have the advantage of being relatively close to the adversary's missile silos. However, the laws of motion require a satellite in low orbit to circle the earth every ninety minutes. After each circuit of the earth, the battle station would be above a different point on the ground, since the earth and the station would be out of step. The station would be within range of an adversary's missile silos only once or twice a day. To cover Soviet missile silos sufficiently, a large number of battle stations indeed would have to be put into orbit: according to the Union of Concerned Scientists, the minimum would be 300 — assuming that all of them worked perfectly.

Geo-stationary battle stations, on the other hand, would always be above their targets, but they would also be forty times farther away than stations in low orbits. This tremendous distance between satellite and target would eliminate the power of any known space weapons to destroy missiles in their boost phase.

An alternative under consideration is to build earth-based lasers whose beams would bounce off relay mirrors in synchronous orbits at an altitude of about 22,300 miles. The relay mirrors would direct the beams to various "fighting" mirrors orbiting the earth at lower altitudes, from which the beams would be directed to their targets. This hybrid system has an advantage in that it puts fewer vulnerable parts in orbit. However, it too faces several severe and unavoidable technical and operational challenges. The directed light beams would have to travel a very great distance. The mirrors would have to be kept optically perfect and capable of changing their angles in fractions of a second under the direction either of their own sensors or of battle-management satellites. Any comprehensive scheme would require mirrors 328 feet across, although the best current optical science can do is create mirrors less than seventeen feet wide for the largest telescopes. MIT physicist Kosta Tsipis states flatly: "Making such a mirror sufficiently rugged and of the necessary optical quality ... is beyond the technical capabilities of the U.S. or any other nation."

Since pre-positioned mirrors would be easy targets, some thought is being given to mirrors that would be carried "collapsed" on rockets. The mirrors would be "popped up" at the first warning of an enemy attack. These mirrors, or interceptors, would have to reach their designated altitude during the boost stage of the enemy missiles — about three to five minutes. Since the earth is round, these weapons would have to be fired from submarines off Siberia or close to the Soviet Union; from Alaska, a Soviet silo in Siberia cannot be seen by the interceptor weapon until it has been projected to an altitude of 620 miles — by which time Soviet missiles would have completed their boost phase. To flash instructions from Washington to submarines in the first moments of nuclear war would be difficult, even assuming the submarines, held in fixed location, had not been found and sunk by Soviets in advance of a nuclear attack. Only one directed-energy weapon has been proposed that would be light enough to be "popped up" into space after a Soviet missile launch had been detected. This is the X-ray laser powered by nuclear explosion. However, as a U.S. Office of Technology Assessment report has pointed out, X-rays from this weapon could not penetrate far into the atmosphere, and a "fast-burn" booster could be designed to release its warheads below this level. All laser beams have trouble cutting through the atmosphere quickly enough to destroy missiles in their boost phase, and X-ray lasers are among the least penetrating. They could hit missiles only at the top of the boost phase, and probably could be used for post-boost or mid-course interception. But that is when the warheads (no longer missiles) are hardest to find because they are hidden amid swarms of decoys.

All pop-up interception schemes, no matter what kind of anti-missile weapon they employ, depend on the assumption that the USSR will not be able to build missiles with a boost phase so short that no pop-up system could view the burning booster. Once the boost phase is completed and the missile is in mid-course, the target to be destroyed is no longer a single missile. One Soviet SS-18 might release ten or more warheads with a hundred or more decoys and quantities of other so-called penetration aids, such as chaff and clouds of aerosol which emit infra-red light. Thus a thousand Soviet launching silos could present U.S. defenses with hundreds of thousands of potential targets. There is also the possible so-called third phase or terminal defense, which means destroying the warheads after they re-enter the atmosphere and come as close as a quarter of a mile to the target. But the Soviets could set their warheads to detonate as soon as they sense interception, and even ten miles away, interception could devastate the cities that Star Wars is trying to protect.

To be effective, any Star Wars system would require massive advances in detection, tracking and "battle-management" technologies. The automated battle-management system necessary to any SDI program

Can Star Wars Work? 171

involves the development of computer hardware and software that can take on the tracking data, assign each missile to the closest battle station and reassign it as it moves out of range, keep the beams on target, verify kills, and figure out where the next nearest targets are. This would require data processing so fast and complicated that a new generation of supercomputers would be needed. Its software would require up to 100 million lines of computer code, written and debugged by as yet undeveloped artificial intelligence systems.

And no complex computer system works right the first time. For example, in the first field trial of Aegis, a computerized system designed to defend naval ships from air attack, the weapon failed to stop six of sixteen targets. Aegis' faulty software was eventually debugged, but for the Star Wars program there may be no second chance.

Many computer researchers have serious concerns about this aspect of SDI. A notable example is David Parnas, an American professor at the University of Victoria who worked with the Naval Research Laboratory, beginning in 1972, helping to develop battle computer programs for the Navy. Parnas was appointed to a Star Wars computer advisory panel. But after attending the first meeting in June of 1985 and studying the problems involved, he turned in a letter of resignation. "Because of the extreme demands on the system and our inability to test it, we will never be able to believe, with any confidence, that we have succeeded," he wrote. "Most of the money spent will be wasted." Forty members of the University of Toronto's computer science department signed a letter to the Canadian government in 1985, stating, in part:

> The computer capabilities required by the Strategic Defense Initiative are beyond any current or reason-

ably foreseeable computer science techniques.... No large computer system has ever been error-free. In addition, experience with false alerts has shown that human judgment is crucial in preventing the accidental launch of nuclear weapons. This is a life-and-death judgment: we do not allow computers to render life-and-death judgments now, nor is it reasonable to allow them to do so in the near future.

The consensus within the scientific community is that a 100 per cent leak-proof umbrella is not possible. To build a totally effective ballistic missile defense, the United States would have to repeal Murphy's law (if anything can go wrong, it will). Incidents like one that took place in June of 1985 show this is about as likely as repealing the law of gravity. Scientists at a U.S. Air Force ground station located on a mountaintop on the Hawaiian island of Maui fired a laser beam 220 miles through space at a minute target, an eight-inch mirror attached to a hatch window of the space shuttle Discovery, which was speeding above the island at 17,500 m.p.h. The intention was to bounce the low-powered ribbon of light off the mirror and send it flashing back to Maui. But while the laser beam successfully "painted" the spacecraft, no reflection bounced back. The scientists had been informed of the height of the mountain, in feet. But the program dealt in nautical miles (which is how Americans measure airplane distance). It did not occur to the scientists that a mountain height of 9,000 miles is unlikely; they went ahead and oriented the shuttle accordingly. It took a second test to get it right.

Critics of Star Wars seized on the initial snafu as proof of the SDI program's folly. Said physicist Robert Bowman, president of the Institute for Space and Security Studies: "The problem is in applications of an immensely complex system.... The chances are that [it] never could be debugged."

Two former U.S. secretaries of defense, Harold Brown and Robert McNamara, agree that it is probably not possible to create technological immunity to Soviet attack. Brown points out that all of the extraordinarily complex systems, computer and otherwise, would have to work perfectly the first time they were tried in combat and that they would have to perform tasks that are well beyond current technology (for example, laser densities "perhaps a million or more times greater than anything that has been achieved" would be required).

Various analogies are made in defense of SDI: people also said it would be impossible to fly in an aircraft, or to go to the moon, or to create accurate intercontinental ballistic missiles. But all these were judgments as to whether one could do something that seemed contrary to nature, and nature does not fight back. As prominent American scientist Richard Garwin, a former member of the president's Science Advisory Committee, has noted in reply to such analogies: "The moon is not suddenly jerked out of the way.... One must ask whether these technically feasible things, assumed feasible, will in fact be useful. The answer is no, because even the same technologies are better used to defeat the defenses than to defend."

Countermeasures

In 1983, Dr. Richard DeLauer, then the Pentagon's top scientist, testified that fulfilment of the objectives of the Star Wars project would require breakthroughs in eight key technologies, each "equivalent or greater than the Manhattan Project" (the World War II atomic bomb effort). America did not undertake the Manhattan Project at a time when the other side was frantically seeking to develop countermeasures. Any Star Wars defense the U.S. might someday develop, at exorbitant cost, would quickly become a depreciating investment. The Soviets will never sit idly by watching America build a shield behind which — as they saw it — Washington might safely launch a first strike. According to Noel Gayler, retired U.S. admiral and former director of the National Security Agency, Star Wars enthusiasts are duped by the "fallacy of the last move" — that is, the notion that Washington can construct this defense system without prompting countermeasures by the opposition. The Soviets "are going to do everything they can to maintain their offensive capability," argues Henry Kendall, an MIT physicist and chairman of the Union of Concerned Scientists. "That's exactly what we did years ago when they started building their ABM (anti-ballistic missile) system. We found out there are a lot of ways you can outfox these things."

The USSR can respond with comparatively cheap and simple means. For example, according to a U.S. congressional report, the Soviets could coat their rockets with a thin heat shield to triple the energy the rocket could absorb before being damaged. If heat shielding tripled the "dwell" time, the report said, lasers would have to be made three times as powerful or three times as many orbiting battle stations would be needed to handle all attacking missiles. Another method of "hardening" a missile, say Star Wars critics, would be to spin it in flight, increasing the area touched by the laser beam and, once again, tripling the required dwell time. But advocates of Star Wars hope that lasers will be powerful enough to burn into a missile's skin in a fraction of a second, so that a rocket could not spin fast enough to avoid a fatal accumulation of heat. Yet if the Soviets adopted both shielding and spinning, with the result (using the same crude math) that the missiles would be nine times harder, a laser would require sixty-three seconds of dwell time to kill a rocket. In other words, lasers would have to be nine times more powerful than they are now in order to kill a rocket with seven seconds of dwell time.

In addition, boost times could be greatly shortened, perhaps to as little as fifty seconds, by equipping missiles with more powerful rocket thrusters and toughening their skins to withstand a faster trip through the atmosphere. Unclassified studies presented to Reagan's Defense Technologies Study Team headed by Dr. James C. Fletcher (the Fletcher panel) calculate that such a rapid burn, lasting only about one minute, would require the missile's payload to be reduced by only ten to fifteen per cent. A related countermeasure would be altering the trajectory of the launch, depressing it so as to complete the rocket's burn below sixty miles. Because the lower atmosphere is opaque to X-ray beams, missiles of high thrust could complete their boost before they could be attacked.

Another comparatively simple ploy would be blinding U.S. sensors by shining a ground-based laser beam up at them. The Soviets could also launch swarms of dummy rockets to distract some sensors and beam weapons, letting more real missiles slip through. These phony re-entry vehicles — lightweight, foil-coated balloons released from the "bus" to coast weightlessly just like hydrogen bombs — are considered by both sides to pose one of the toughest countermeasures a Star Wars system could confront. Testifying before the House Armed Services Committee, Richard DeLauer, then under-secretary of defense for research and engineering, stated that "any defense system can be overcome with proliferation and decoys, decoys, decoys." "Just imagine what you'd be faced with," says MIT's Henry Kendall, "They could give each decoy the ability to manoeuvre and emit spurious radar signals. You'd have a million objects manoeuvring, sizzling and sparkling. All they need is wristwatch electronics to run all this. You'd have to shoot at everything."

Even if the whole system for killing missiles and re-entry vehicles could be built, one major problem would remain: how to prevent the Soviets from knocking out the battle stations or sensor satellites just before launching their missiles. Critics say that the Soviets could easily put up "space mines" to orbit parallel to U.S. battle stations but circling in the opposite direction. Then at zero hour a radio signal would nudge a space mine into the battle station's path, causing a collision that would shatter both. "Many potential counters, such as decoys or space mines, have the power to neutralize space-based systems," says Stanford University physicist and arms control expert Sidney Drell. His colleague Arthur Schawlow, who won the Nobel Prize for his work on developing the laser, agrees: "A laser battle station out in open space would be a sitting duck."

Obviously then, the first step in any Soviet plan to launch a missile attack would be to destroy or disable U.S. directed-energy weapons. This could be done in a variety of ways with relative ease. The cheapest methods would use anti-satellite weapons to jam communications links to U.S. ground control centres, or detonate nuclear weapons in space to produce an electromagnetic pulse [E.M.P.] that would burn out communications systems. The president's Fletcher panel report admitted that the "survivability of the system components is a critical issue whose resolution requires a combination of technologies and tactics that remain to be worked out."

But the simplest Soviet countermeasure of all would be a massive build-up of offensive nuclear warheads in an attempt to overwhelm SDI — the opposite of what President Reagan promises. Even pro-Reagan Europeans are concerned about allocating scarce resources to a program that could create what British Foreign Secretary Sir Geoffrey Howe has called "a Maginot Line of the 21st century" — a reference to the tragically overrated French defense fortification of the Second World War.

All these Soviet countermeasures would exploit available technology, but the space defense would rely on unproven technologies. But the Soviets could also take advantage of many of the projected SDI technologies themselves to sabotage a Star Wars system. As William Perry, former U.S. under-secretary of defense for research and engineering, has stated:

> It can be fairly said that I am a technological optimist, and the view I am expressing is based on a pretty optimistic assessment of the technology involved. It is quite correct that this technology can be used to develop strategic defenses; the problem is that it can equally well be used by the side trying to defeat or degrade those defenses. In a measure-countermeasure game, technology is a two-edged sword. For example, advances in laser technology could also enable an attacker to penetrate a defense. Developments in computers that could help manage defenses could just as easily manage effective countermeasures.

Another problem with a space-based ballistic missile defense is that it does not defend against weapons that fly below the upper atmosphere, such as terrain-hugging Cruise missiles, low-flying bombers or depressed-trajectory (low re-entry angle) ballistic missiles. These weapons are certain to become a major part of Soviet strategic forces once missile defense systems appear on the horizon. (The implications of such deployments for Canadian defense will be discussed in the next chapter.)

Among all the dozens of spokespeople for the Reagan administration there is not one with any significant technical qualifications who has been willing to question Richard DeLauer's explicit statement: "There is no way an enemy can't overwhelm your defenses if he wants to badly enough." On strictly technical terms, Star Wars is fundamentally flawed. As a study released by the Congressional Office of Technology Assessment concluded in April of 1984: "The prospect that emerging 'Star Wars' technologies, when further developed, will provide a perfect or near-perfect defense system ... is so remote that it should not serve as the basis of public expectation or national policy."

Yet, as we'll see in the next chapter, the daunting technical problems faced by the Star Wars idea do not spell its demise.

7
Allies in Wonderland

While the prospect of space-based warfare is frightening, it is also saddening. For this is one aspect of the arms race that the superpowers have, until recently, enjoyed some success in controlling. This chapter will look at the background of the role of space in the arms race (including Soviet "Star Wars"), and then turn to the possible offensive uses of a Star Wars defense system. Finally, Canada's involvement in SDI will be discussed.

The ABM Treaty

In military jargon, the Star Wars scheme would be an anti-ballistic missile (ABM) system. While early ABM plans were based on land rather than in space, the dangers were similar. In the early 1970s, nationwide ABM defenses were judged to be:

- futile, because in a competition between offensive missiles and defensive systems, the offense would win, especially against urban areas;
- destabilizing, first because they would speed up the arms race as both sides developed and deployed not only defensive systems, but also offensive systems to overpower, evade, or attack and disable the opposing ABM defense; second, because each side would fear the purpose or the capability of the other's ABM defenses (especially against a weakened retal-

iatory strike), and in a crisis these fears might create pressure to strike first;
- costly, because the offensive countermeasures taken by the other side to maintain its deterrent threat of intolerable retaliatory damage appeared not only capable of overwhelming the defense, but also less costly.

In what must now seem like a perverse irony, it was the Soviets, not the Americans, who were the early advocates of ballistic-missile defense (BMD). Indeed, in the late 1960s the issue was a major stumbling block to the initiation of talks on limiting strategic nuclear arms. The Soviets insisted that defensive missiles were good because they destroyed weapons, not people, and that only offensive systems should be constrained. The Americans argued that any BMD produced by known technology could be overwhelmed readily by an increase in the number and sophistication of offensive warheads, and would only stimulate offensive and defensive arms races. U.S. Defense Secretary Robert McNamara and President Lyndon Johnson managed to persuade Soviet Prime Minister Aleksei Kosygin that the first nation to achieve both offensive and defensive capabilities might well be tempted to launch a devastating nuclear first strike. Thus began talks that led eventually to an ABM Treaty; its preamble noted that "effective measures to limit anti-ballistic missile systems would be a substantial factor in curbing the race in strategic offensive arms and would lead to a decrease in the risk of outbreak of war involving nuclear weapons."

The treaty, signed in 1972, defines ABM systems as those which "counter strategic ballistic missiles or their elements in flight trajectory" and includes new technologies such as lasers. The treaty permits deployment of only one limited, land-based anti-ballistic missile system; it explicitly prohibits the development, testing, or deployment of any space-based ABM system or component. In Article V, "each party undertakes not to develop, test, or deploy ABM systems or components which are sea-based, air-based, space-based or mobile land-based." The fundamental premise underlying the ABM treaty was that nuclear war is not survivable, that a search for technological solutions contrary to this reality would not only be futile, but dangerous. This assumption remains valid today. The treaty has contributed to maintaining the peace for over a decade.

The SDI is not confined to research permitted by the ABM Treaty. In fact it emphasizes the development and demonstration of prototype ABM weapons in violation of the ABM treaty. In National Security Decision Directive No. 119, which established the Strategic Defense Initiative, President Reagan gave the Department of Defense a mandate to "demonstrate" defensive weapons technology — a word that covers the grey area between research and development. Under standard U.S. military practice, demonstration entails activities that go well beyond research and clearly involve the display of weapons prototypes. Research on "sub-components," if it involves the actual testing of experimental devices in outer space, may be indistinguishable from development. In June of 1985, for example, the U.S. space shuttle participated in a test of an earth-based laser beam, which was fired at a reflector on the shuttle Discovery. While the Defense Department described the demonstration as an element of research related to studies of how light spreads in space, critics of SDI pointed out that general physics were already well understood. The "experiment" looked more like a demonstration of how to track and destroy an object in space.

The chief negotiator of the ABM treaty, Gerard Smith, has said that the SDI places the United States in "anticipatory breach" of the agreement. "Research," according to the Canadian Centre for Arms Control and Disarmament, "is not inherently pristine in character or in its real-world effects. It is clear that the current U.S. administration does not see the SDI as a routine research activity. The SDI is clearly a crash program to identify a technological path to cost-effective strategic defenses." Recently announced U.S. funding and testing plans add to the fear that the guiding emphasis of SDI has become the demonstration and early deployment of technologically feasible elements of the program. Washington will break the letter of the agreement if it places its research program on the schedule implied by Lt. Gen. James Abrahamson, when he said in March of 1985 that a "reasonably confident decision" on whether to build Star Wars could be made by the end of the decade or in the early 1990s.

If the U.S. is unwilling to refrain from the tests associated with such a schedule, the Soviets will, with good reason, assume that Washington is preparing to deploy strategic defenses. The Soviet response will probably be one of increasing their nuclear arsenal to counter the American SDI. "The choice," according to Lawrence Hagen, director of research with the Canadian Centre for Arms Control and Disarmament, "is not simply 'Star Wars' or no 'Star Wars'. It is also 'Star Wars' or arms control." Indeed, many of the people who have latched on to SDI in the U.S. are interested in destroying the arms control process itself.

Abandonment of the ABM Treaty would result in an unrestrained competition in strategic defense systems, the weaponization of space, a rapid escalation in offensive nuclear weapons, and the erosion of hope for progress in any arms control negotiations. Spurgeon Keeny, Jr., deputy of the U.S. Arms Control and Disarmament Agency from 1977 to 1981, has perhaps best summed up the implications:

> If the United States, having failed to ratify the SALT II agreement, decides to withdraw from the ABM Treaty either unilaterally or by agreement, the death knell will have sounded for arms control for the foreseeable future. This will be a high price to pay for a technological will-o'-the-wisp that can only lead us into the swamp of an endless and dangerous high-technology arms race.

Anti-satellite Weapons

While the ABM Treaty banned space-based defense systems, space has not been untouched by the arms race. Both superpowers have long relied on satellites for surveillance and communication. Now, accompanying Star Wars technology in the militarization of space, there is a move by both the United States and the Soviet Union to develop and deploy anti-satellite weapons (ASATs). ASATs are designed to destroy the opposing side's "eyes and ears" in a bid to "prevail" in a nuclear war. The existing generation of ASATs is very limited. Most of the satellites that the military of both countries rely on for warning of attack, for communications with strategic forces, and for navigation support functions are located at an altitude ten times higher than the range of current ASAT systems. But the next generation of ASATs assuredly will place vital satellites at risk.

184 Misguided Missiles

The USSR began developing an ASAT capability in the mid-1960s and conducted a series of tests which were suspended in 1971 but resumed in 1976. Based on the SS-9 ICBM booster, the Soviet ASAT involves launching into orbit a conventional non-nuclear explosive device which reaches its target after one or two revolutions of orbit. It is clear from available information that the Soviet "killer satellite" is a weapon of limited capabilities. It has a test reliability record of only about fifty per cent, and has been characterized by Air Force Chief of Staff Lew Allen as "having a very questionable operational capacity." It does potentially threaten low-flying U.S. space assets, including photographic reconnaissance satellites and the Transit navigation satellites, but knowledgeable observers estimate that the Soviet ASATs would require well in excess of a week to destroy all such U.S. satellites. The most important U.S. satellites, such as those used for early warning and communications, are in orbit at about 22,300 miles — far beyond the demonstrated range of the Soviet ASAT. And the threat posed by the current Soviet ASAT to American satellites in lower orbits will decline in coming years, as various survivability programs are implemented. For example, the navigation support mission will be transferred to the Navstar satellites, which orbit at an altitude of 12,400 miles. There have been reports of Soviet follow-on systems but there is little evidence that the capability of Soviet anti-satellite systems has improved substantially.

The U.S. is not new to the development of antisatellite weapons. Its Air Force first tested an antisatellite weapon successfully in October of 1959 when an ASAT missile, launched from a B-47 aircraft, intercepted an Explorer 6 satellite which had been set up as a target. Between 1964 and 1975, the U.S. had an operational anti-satellite system based at Johnson Atoll, 60 miles southwest of Hawaii. It consisted of an Air Force Thor missile armed with a nuclear warhead. Recently, the Reagan administration has cited Moscow's possession of an ASAT as justification for developing a much more advanced, small, highly accurate, less verifiable ASAT which can ascend to higher altitudes. Rather than attempting to restrain its research and development programs to a level commensurate with the existing Soviet weapon, Washington plans to deploy ten times the number of Soviet systems.

The U.S. ASAT system, now under advanced development and testing, involves the launching of a small two-stage rocket interceptor from an F-15 aircraft. As a small missile launched from a relatively small airplane, it would give virtually no warning to Soviet radars or satellites that an attack was imminent. The U.S. system, unlike the Soviet system, needs no specialized missile launching pad: if the Air Force wanted to, it could launch many ASATs from many locations in a very short period of time — and much more cheaply than the Soviets could. Because of the system's small size there would be no way for the Soviet Union to verify the number deployed. Every F-15 would be a potential ASAT launcher, since the rocket could be attached in about six hours. This system is not only faster and more flexible than its Soviet counterpart, but its homing technique is more difficult to foil. It will, however, only be capable of hitting targets in low orbit — although a significant number of crucial Soviet strategic satellites operate within range. The Congressional Office of Technology Assessment concluded in 1984: "The U.S. air-launched ASAT weapon now undergoing testing is clearly technically superior to the present generation of Soviet ground-launched ASATs."

The research underway on U.S. ASATs is attempting to overcome their short range, and the best means to do so may include more advanced ground- and air-launched interceptors based on conventional explosives, the addition of more stages to the rocket, and the use of laser weapons. The close integration of the anti-satellite system with NORAD is illustrated by a comment of General James Hartinger, commander in chief of NORAD: "These F-15s will be both fighter-interceptors in support of NORAD air-defense mission and they'll be the launch vehicles in our anti-satellite system." Canadian Armed Forces officials will neither confirm nor deny that 1984 ASAT tests involved the space-tracking station in St. Margarets, New Brunswick.

It is clear that the new U.S. ASAT system is not the last word in weapons of this sort. In the absence of negotiated restraint, both the U.S. and the USSR are likely to develop even more capable anti-satellite weapons, which will share two disturbing characteristics: the ability to attack satellites in high orbits, and an increasing resemblance to anti-ballistic missile systems. If this development is not forestalled it will effectively mark the end of the period when space can be regarded as a sanctuary for communication and observation. (It was the seriousness of this development that led Prime Minister Trudeau, in November of 1983, to propose that negotiations to agree on a specific ban of high altitude ASATs begin immediately.)

What role would anti-satellite weapons play in nuclear war? According to a study by the U.S. Congressional Office of Technology Assessment, the sensors and communications links upon which an ASAT system depends are not likely to survive an initial nuclear attack. Therefore:

> an attack on satellites ... seems practical only for the side that is planning to strike first.... The fact that attacks on early warning and communications satellites would be most useful to the side which started what it expected would be a protracted nuclear war makes for additional crisis instability.

The ability to knock out key communications and early-warning satellites will create first-strike incentives, with the superpowers possibly seeking to pre-empt each other in a crisis situation before losing their satellite systems. Both sides might feel impelled in a crisis to "blind or be blinded." Eugene Carroll has noted that "By offering yet another incentive to strike first, before crucial satellite systems are disrupted, anti-satellite systems will put the nuclear hair-trigger on an even finer edge." That trigger could too easily be pulled in error, perhaps after an incident of the type that took place in 1975, when U.S. satellites mistook a Soviet pipeline fire for an ASAT laser attack. Daniel Deudney of the Worldwatch Institute warns: "The Archduke Francis Ferdinand of World War III may well be a critical U.S. or Soviet reconnaissance satellite hit by a piece of space junk during a crisis."

Another way that a major conflict might be set off is if attacks on spy or early-warning satellites are regarded not only as an act of war but as the first step in a major — probably nuclear — assault. According to defense expert and long-time Pentagon consultant Richard Garwin, "War in space is not an alternative to war on earth but a *prelude* to war on earth." An

ASAT attack on either country's military satellites, even if only partially "blinding" the enemy to possible ICBM attack, would by itself be likely to prompt the blinded nation to launch nuclear missiles. The destabilizing dangers of ASAT development would be increased even more in the context of Star Wars since strategic defense systems would be dependent on satellites.

The United States could have achieved a mutual moratorium on the testing of anti-satellite missiles. Soviet leaders, eager to prevent a quantum leap in U.S. space warfare technology, initiated a unilateral moratorium on the testing of Soviet ASATs in August of 1983. At that time, the U.S. claimed that verification was impossible, but refused to begin talks to work out ways to improve verification. Could the Soviets cheat on an ASAT agreement by secretly testing new weapons? President Reagan has claimed that they could, but experts disagree. Notes Leslie Dirks, former CIA deputy director for research and technology: "I'm quite confident that testing things in space is a hard thing to do, and the United States has a very robust detection capability in this area." The U.S. maintains and is currently upgrading an elaborate system of space radars and advanced optical telescopes designed to track orbiting objects as small as several square inches in size, and eventually to observe football-sized objects in geo-synchronous orbit. Computers at the North American Aerospace Defense Command headquarters will soon be able to track thousands of objects at one time. There is little doubt that the U.S. is able to verify a soundly drafted ASAT space weapons ban. James Reynolds, a former official in the space division of the U.S. Air Force and now a manager of aerospace activities for the Northrop Corporation, has recently argued: "The people who postulate this threat [Soviet ASAT cheating] don't know a spacecraft from a frying pan. It is highly improbable."

Yet if the Reagan administration conducts further ASAT tests, Washington will irrecoverably pass the point where verification of a ban on such weapons is most feasible. The U.S. appears to have two motives for refusing to negotiate the ban. First, the U.S. is considerably ahead of the Soviets in ASAT technology. Second, the kind of weapons used in ASATs are similar enough to those that would be used in the new SDI systems that a ban on one could mean a ban on the other. Walter Slocombe, when a defense official in the Carter administration, said: "A serious treaty limiting anti-satellite weapons technology is not consistent with a no-holds-barred ABM research, development and test program." As it stands, the U.S. can circumvent the present ABM Treaty and get away with testing ABM technology like the ground-based excimer laser by claiming that it is an ASAT weapon, which, indeed, it could also serve as.

Soviet "Star Wars"

As early as the 1950s, American leaders became concerned that the Soviets might be developing an effective ABM system to neutralize U.S. offensive weapons. Officials were alarmed at overstated intelligence reports that Soviet installations with the quaint name of Galosh were being built to protect Moscow and that the Tallinn air-defense system was really designed to knock down attacking ballistic missiles. Today the Pentagon bolsters its claim for new missions and resources by exaggerating reports of Soviet progress toward missile defenses.

The American Star Wars initiative has been endorsed by some as a "prudent" response to a Soviet ABM program. As Brian Mulroney put it when announcing his SDI decision: "Only a naive six-year-old would fail to understand that the Americans are involved in this research because the Soviets have been doing it for a long period of time." According to Western observers, the Soviet Union has been actively pursuing a ballistic missile defense capability. The Soviets continue to operate a BMD installation around Moscow (as permitted by the ABM Treaty), and they have upgraded the system through a continuing research and development program. They are also completing a phased-array radar system in central Siberia that apparently will violate the ABM Treaty. This radar system is perfectly positioned to defend Soviet SS-18 and SS-19 silos against incoming American warheads. However, this potential Soviet capability to track incoming warheads in their terminal phase is by itself of marginal military significance. The U.S. Air Force's own phased-array radar warning system, known as Pavepaws, is more advanced, and the Homing Overlay Experiment (in which for the first time a test missile outside the earth's atmosphere was tracked and destroyed) showed that U.S. warhead tracking is generally far ahead of anything the Soviets have tested.

While the Soviet Union's recent efforts for space arms control seem genuinely motivated by the fear of being buried by an avalanche of American high-tech wizardry, the Russians have not been laggards in pursuing laser ABM technology. A recent U.S. Department of Defense report to Congress claims that the Soviets have been working "as long as and more intensively than the U.S." on directed-energy weapons, have "built more than six large research facilities and test ranges for these weapons ... and are developing chemical laser and ... gas dynamic and electric discharge lasers." In 1983, U.S. officials charged that "at least two major malfunctions" of U.S. satellites were due to illumination from Soviet ground-based lasers and that a third "may be due to foul play." In its comprehensive 1983 annual report, *The Soviet Year in Space*, the aerospace corporation Teledyne Brown says the Soviets could field a space-based laser ASAT by the late 1980s and a test laser ABM as soon as the early 1990s. While the sources for such claims demand close scrutiny, it would not be uncharacteristic — given the Soviet Union's propensity for deploying weapons earlier in the development cycle than the U.S. — for the USSR to orbit some sort of limited-capability laser weapon before the U.S. does.

The Pentagon claims that the U.S. needs to catch up with the Soviets in SDI technology. After having disposed of the bomber gap and the missile gap, the U.S. now faces an anti-missile gap! Again the gap is real — but it is the U.S. that is at least a decade ahead of the Soviets in ABM technology. There have been no developments in Soviet ABM capabilities that would justify the American Star Wars program. As U.S. Secretary of Defense Harold Brown noted in 1981: "Although the Soviets may be investigating the application of high energy lasers and even charged particle beams ... severe technical obstacles remain in the way of converting this technology into a weapon system that would have any practical capability against missiles." According to the Union of Concerned Scientists, the Soviet BMD program seems to be quite similar to that of the U.S. before the SDI initiative began: "We know of no evidence that they are moving toward a comprehensive strategic defense of Soviet society." As the Fletcher panel emphasized, the most daunting SDI problems are computer-intensive, and that is an area in which the Soviets are exceptionally weak. Indeed, the Soviets lag in almost all technologies critical to space-based BMD. A 1983 internal Pentagon report showed that the U.S. is equal to the Soviet Union in directed-energy technology, but "superior in virtually every other technology needed to fashion a working anti-ballistic missile system, including computers, optics, automated control, electro-optical sensors, microelectronics, propulsion, radar, signal processing, software, telecommunications, and guidance systems."

American SDI research is not merely an attempt to keep up with Soviet anti-missile advances and avoid being taken by surprise. The announcement in late 1984 that U.S. aiming and tracking tests devised for defensive weapons will be accelerated by two years shows that SDI is actually a crash program to achieve invulnerability to nuclear missiles. Of course, the U.S. cannot sit idle and permit a possible Soviet "breakout" from research to deployment of anti-missile systems. But before the SDI declaration, Washington was spending sufficient dollars on BMD research (approximately $1 billion a year) to act as a hedge against Soviet ABM break-out. The current American $26-billion research program is a crash program which aims at an *American* break-out.

SDI: Its Effectiveness and Effects

As we saw in the last chapter, the likelihood of a "Star Wars" scheme providing the sort of impermeable barrier promised by President Reagan is slight. What, then, are the consequences of creating a "leaky" umbrella? One hundred cities would still be destroyed if only two per cent of Soviet nuclear weapons were able to reach North American soil. According to the U.S. Arms Control and Disarmament Agency, "A defense that was 95% effective could result in 60 million deaths and a 98% effective defense could cause 40 million deaths."

A common Pentagon fall-back position is that even a partially effective defense would introduce a vital element of uncertainty into Soviet attack plans and would thereby enhance deterrence. But this justification fails for the simple reason that, as President Reagan's Scowcroft Commission confirmed, the U.S. strategic triad of land-, sea-, and air-launched nuclear weapons is already sufficiently invulnerable to deny the Soviet Union the capacity for a disarming first strike.

A perfect defense would carry its own dangers. Progress toward Star Wars deployment is most unlikely to be symmetrical. As one superpower approached the point where its anti-missile system seemed about to become operative, the risk of conflict could increase dramatically. The other nation would certainly feel threatened by the realization that much of its offensive arsenal would shortly be neutralized. The tenuous balance of mutual vulnerability would be upset. Neither the U.S. nor the USSR could afford to let the other side become invulnerable; such a concession would be seen as virtual surrender. The other side could attack with impunity. Kurt Gottfried, a Cornell physicist and defense consultant, has said of SDI that "If such a system can be constructed, it is the equivalent of putting all the other side's ICBMs in the garbage can; therefore they won't allow it to happen." Ironically, the nation that deploys missile defense first could pay a great price for its efforts without reaping any return. Preemption could trigger the nuclear conflict that devastates the earth.

Even small improvements in the ability of one country to penetrate the adversary's defense are extremely sensitive. Because modern technology never stands still, a strategic defense system could never be consistently perfect, only temporarily impenetrable. Both sides would be left scrambling to penetrate the other's defenses, and whoever was initially successful might have a powerful incentive to attack while the other was vulnerable. Rather than rest relatively secure in the knowledge that retaliation is possible (and hence understand the need for arms control), each side would have every reason to mistrust the other and to develop new weapons. As Kosta Tsipis explains:

> In the face of a determined and capable opponent, the survivability of any spaceborne weapon will depend on short-lived technical advantages over the opponent's system. This survivability will evaporate as improvements are made by the enemy. The confidence in the survivability of one's system will improve again as counter-improvements are implemented to combat the enemy's measures. Thus, spaceborne weapons systems are subject to *technological instability*, i.e., they will be faced with frequent crises of vulnerability that would have to be remedied promptly. The countermeasures and counter-countermeasures cycle promises to be rapid and endless.

The very technical sophistication that makes SDI conceivable would, if the defense were realized, make it vulnerable and laden with danger. The rapid response requirements of SDI would further destabilize the nuclear peace because they would increasingly place the superpowers' nuclear arsenals on a hair-trigger. As the International Institute of Strategic Studies noted: "When deployed, some elements of the defenses ... have to be programmed to react within a very few minutes, thus decreasing time for human judgment to influence the firing process." Given that even a partially effective SDI must be able to destroy enemy missiles in their boost phase, sophisticated computers would increasingly be relied upon both to determine whether or not a nuclear conflict had commenced and to unleash the "appropriate" response. "It is hard to conceive of a boost-phase intercept without a heavy reliance on computers," says James Fletcher, the former NASA chief who headed Reagan's panel to study SDI feasibility, "so it would have to be primarily automatic." But as we saw in the previous chapter, defense computers can break down or make mistakes as easily as other computers. The computer hardware might seem to work flawlessly while crippling software errors lurked undetected in the system. "No one who knows about missile-defense systems would put the survivability of such systems in the hands of computers," says Richard Garwin. "It's like a whole bunch of sparking switches in a gasoline-filled room. The least error in that computer system would launch a nuclear war."

It has become apparent even to the government's scientists that no technology can provide an absolute shield. An impenetrable defense is no longer the U.S. administration's actual goal for SDI, despite Reagan's and Weinberger's continuing protestations to the contrary. "A perfect astrodome defense is not a realistic thing," Lt. Gen. Abrahamson, head of the Strategic Defense Initiative Project Office, acknowledged in 1984. Although paying lip service to presidential orthodoxy whenever they can remember to do so, most U.S. administration spokesmen quietly reject the idea that SDI will defend the cities or relieve the need to rely on nuclear deterrence. But the Pentagon can still find uses — such as "point defense" and support of a first use — for a leaky umbrella. These will be discussed in turn.

Point Defense

Current SDI efforts are elements of strategic modernization programs that are not based on the protection of populations. They are based on the protection of weapon systems within an environment of what some U.S. military and political leaders believe could be prolonged (and limited) nuclear war. As under-secretary of defense for policy Fred Ikle remarked at a secret session of the Senate Armed Services Committee, "As you move toward deployment of the full system, there are some intermediate steps which have intermediate utility.... Components of a multi-tiered defense could become deployed earlier than a complete system."

Those components relate to what is known as "point defense," a combination of highly developed radar, infra-red sensors, interceptor missiles, and so on, that would protect specific ICBM sites and associated command and control centres by intercepting incoming warheads within the atmosphere or just outside it. A U.S. Defense Department pamphlet published in April of 1984 predicted that point defense could be available between 1990 and 2000. At first glance, point defense does seem much more "realistic" than Star Wars. Unlike Star Wars, point defense is technically feasible and probably attainable in the near term.

Point defenses are, however, quickly being absorbed into war-fighting and limited nuclear war scenarios.

Even a partially effective defense against incoming missiles would add to the survivability of the war-fighting weapons being developed as part of the U.S. strategic modernization program, permitting them to be reserved, within a nuclear war, for what U.S. Defense Secretary Weinberger has called "controlled nuclear attacks over a protracted period." The upgrading of NORAD's ballistic-missile warning systems and the communications systems that connect them with NORAD headquarters in Cheyenne Mountain, Colorado are part of the overall modernization of strategic nuclear weapons and the command, control and intelligence systems that support them. Weapons and their support systems must now be capable of operating amidst the destruction of nuclear war. In the words of the commander in chief of NORAD, General Hartinger, "We at NORAD provide the flexible nuclear response options." Nuclear strategy analyst Desmond Ball explains why U.S. policy required changes to NORAD's facilities: "The command and control requirements of concepts such as flexible response, damage limitation and nuclear war-fighting are obviously more complex and elaborate than those required for a second strike based on a pre-determined set of targets." Point defenses are central to "limited" nuclear war-fighting plans as they permit (in theory, at least) the selective use of nuclear missiles over a sustained period. As Caspar Weinberger puts it: "U.S. strategic nuclear forces and their command and communication links should be capable of supporting controlled nuclear counterattacks over a protracted period while maintaining a reserve of nuclear forces sufficient for trans- and post-attack protection and coercion."

First-strike Options

American defense officials now advocate the integration of limited SDI goals with U.S. offensive nuclear capabilities. The *New York Times* has reported that the Pentagon has devised a plan to bring the Star Wars initiative and the rest of America's nuclear arsenal under a single command structure. This opens up the possibility of a U.S. first-strike option. In the absence of a strategic defense system, U.S. military planners would not be able to give this option much more than passing consideration since an effective strike against land-based weapons would leave Soviet sea-based weapons to launch a counterattack. The threat of mutually assured destruction would hold. But for the superpower with a strategic defense system in place, a first strike in the context of a deeply critical situation becomes a genuine possibility. The side with the advantage might bet everything on what Harold Brown has called "the cosmic roll of the dice" — an attempt to disarm the other side by knocking out its defensive forces. Paul Sayers, a defense analyst specializing in the military uses of outer space at the Brookings Institution, has used the analogy of two warriors armed with swords. One acquires a suit of armour, and with his new-found protection is tempted to strike, knowing he is immune to counterattack. Thinking in these terms, some strategists regard the so-called "defensive" weapons simply as tools for potential aggression. World-famous Russian physicist Andrei Sakharov made this point in 1967 when he discouraged Soviet anti-ballistic missile developments: "The construction of an anti-missile defense system would mean adding a shield to the sword. I think that such an expansion of nuclear missile armaments would be very dangerous.... A shield would increase the lure of nuclear blackmail."

Any attempt to break out of the mutual hostage relationship — either by protecting one's population or by acquiring the capability to carry out a disarming strike against the other side's forces — will be destabilizing. Such actions erode stability by raising the possibility, or at least the perception, that a first strike might confer meaningful strategic advantage. A study published by the U.S. Congressional Office of Technology Assessment in 1985 acknowledged that SDI weapons might increase the temptation of one nation to strike first. "There is great uncertainty," the report concluded, "about the strategic situation that would arise."

A first-strike option is not dependent upon a completely leak-proof umbrella. An SDI-type system would collapse under a full-scale Soviet first strike, but might cope "adequately" with the depleted Soviet forces that had survived an American first strike. "Such a system makes more sense as an adjunct to a first-strike capability than as a shield from a first strike," Princeton physicist Frank von Hippel pointed out in the *Bulletin of Atomic Scientists*. "Because of its inevitable vulnerability, a Star Wars-type system would be fairly easy to neutralize at the beginning of a highly orchestrated first strike. But, in the face of a disorganized retaliatory strike by an unprepared victim of a surprise attack, it might be more effective."

The U.S. Coalition for a New Foreign and Military Policy has calculated that if current American deployment plans are carried out, by 1995 an American first strike against the Soviet Union could leave as few as 700 Soviet warheads available for retaliation. In comparison, a Soviet first strike against the U.S. would leave 4,500 surviving warheads.

Anyone who doubts that a Star Wars deployment is perceived as a threat by the USSR needs only to listen to Caspar Weinberger speaking for the other side. If the Soviets were to build a similar system, he acknowledged, it would be "one of the most frightening prospects" imaginable. Another who recognized the danger is Dr. Robert Bowman. Bowman was director of the U.S. Air Force's Star Wars program, but he resigned to head up the Anti-SDI Institute for Space and Security Studies. His disenchantment with Star Wars was largely due to its first-strike potential:

> There *is* a way that one might make a Star Wars system militarily effective. All you have to do is add one more layer — I call it the "Pre-Boost Phase Defensive Layer." It amounts to destroying enemy ICBMs in their silos *before* they're launched. We have the technology to do that: it's called the MX, Pershing II, and Trident II. Get 90 per cent or so that way and there's a chance that a Star Wars system might actually be of some use against the few that remain. Of course, some people don't think that sounds like defense at all — it sounds like first strike. And they're right!

Through Soviet eyes, the SDI offers ample grounds for an alarming worst-case analysis of the U.S. threat. A U.S. territorial defense, deployed in combination with new hard-target weapons like the MX, Trident II and Pershing II, would undeniably look like a formidable first-strike capability against the land-based missiles that form two-thirds of the Soviet arsenal. This threat can only strengthen the Soviet resolve and paranoia.

A return to innocence, to being the most powerful nation by virtue of either a nuclear monopoly or a defensive shield, appeals to American instincts and corresponds with official hopes. This is how those hopes are summed up by Colin Gray: "In the event that the United States succeeded in deploying a population defense that was technically robust, a considerable measure of U.S. freedom of political action should be restored as a logical consequence." Elsewhere, Gray argues that damage limitation would enhance the credibility of extended deterrence, which is based on the willingness of the United States to use nuclear weapons first: "Logically at least a United States equipped with damage-limiting 'layers' of active and passive defenses should be more willing to take the controlled and limited strategic nuclear initiative on behalf of beleaguered overseas allies." According to this strategy, the reason for deploying a partial missile defense system would not be to undertake a first strike, but to establish escalation dominance, ensuring that in crisis situations throughout the world, the Soviet Union would back down first. Caspar Weinberger has acknowledged that goal: "If we can get a system which is effective and which we know can render their weapons impotent we could be back in a situation we were in, for example, when we were the only nation with a nuclear weapon."

Ernie Regehr of Project Ploughshares has argued that

> while the U.S. Administration may deny and indeed may not have the intention of initiating a nuclear first strike now or in the future, the current strategic modernization program in the U.S. is pursuing first-strike "options" and it is undeniable that the Soviet

Union will perceive the development of first-strike weapons coupled with strategic defense measures as a major threat to their security.

The real risk of nuclear war is not a cold-blooded decision to initiate one, but what might happen under the pressures and suspicions of a crisis. An effective but imperfect space defense system on one side would only serve to exacerbate the risk of war. Similarly, the side without such a defensive system might conclude that its situation would be better, however bad, if it struck first and avoided being caught trying to retaliate with a weakened force against a space-based anti-ballistic missile system. The same calculation would affect both sides if both possessed a Star Wars system. If both the United States and the Soviet Union had partial Star Wars shields in place, the situation would not be more stable; in fact, it would be more threatening. Each side would want to launch its missiles first for fear that it would lose them later.

The Economics of SDI

The defense industry in both the U.S. and Canada has lauded the Strategic Defense Initiative — for good reason. Former U.S. secretaries of defense, Harold Brown and James Schlesinger, and senior Pentagon spokesmen of the current administration have estimated that the full cost of Star Wars will be anywhere from hundreds of billions to one trillion dollars — it would seem the sky's the limit! When a trillion dollars is waved at the U.S. aerospace industry, the project in question will rapidly acquire an economic and institutional life of its own — independent of the validity of its public justifications. With jobs, corporate profits, and civilian and military promotions at stake, a project of this magnitude, once started, becomes a juggernaut, the more difficult to stop the longer it rolls on. A 1984 report from the Council on Economic Priorities in New York shows that a strong constituency is already being created to support the Star Wars research and development program. The top ten Pentagon contractors (Lockheed, McDonnell Douglas, Rockwell International, Boeing, TRW, Litton, etc.) have received 87 per cent of the SDI contracts so far. These are the same contractors who are producing the next generation of first-strike nuclear weapons. They are being paid to assess the feasibility of a system that they will end up building. To slice it another way: almost all the contracts have been awarded to the districts and states of key congressional decision-makers on this issue. Paul Warnke, President Carter's chief SALT II negotiator, refers to SDI as "the great pork barrel in the sky."

A number of Canadian business leaders have suggested that job creation might be the redeeming virtue of Canadian SDI research. Aerospace Industries Association president, Kenneth Lewis, and Thomas Allan, president of Control Data Canada Ltd., have suggested that 50,000 SDI jobs could be generated in Canada by 1992. Two points of caution are noteworthy. First, weapon systems should be judged on their merits alone. Dangerous weapons are not made more acceptable or unacceptable by virtue of their economic impact. Second, the economic benefits of SDI would be much more modest than has been suggested. As economist John Kenneth Galbraith told Prime Minister Mulroney: "Nothing should be regarded with such vulgar suspicion as the notion that Star Wars can create jobs."

As we saw in Chapter 5, defense industry spending is a poor job creator compared to other sectors. The precise number of jobs that Star Wars research could create is uncertain, but according to Ernie Regehr, a reasonable idea might be gained from some recent research and development contracts. An $85 million contract awarded to Spar Aerospace by the U.S. military is said to promise 500 person-years of work, and $2 billion worth of Canadian work on the U.S. space station is expected to generate 9,000 year-long jobs. In both cases, it takes about $200,000 of economic activity to create each job. Following this ratio, $50 million in SDI research could create about 250 Canadian jobs. But what if that $50 million were spent elsewhere? In Canada, $50 million in government job-creation programs could generate more than 1,000 jobs per year. Similarly, an equivalent expenditure by the private sector on civilian production would result in considerably more than 250 jobs.

Two studies have been completed on the number of jobs that could be generated in Canada through SDI. A confidential Spar Aerospace report prepared for the federal Cabinet suggested that Star Wars contracts would probably generate about 1,000 jobs a year in Canada — most of them not for average unemployed Canadians, but for highly skilled scientists, who are already in short supply. A study by the Canadian Centre for Arms Control and Disarmament calculated that approximately 1,680 jobs would be created per year in Canada, but only just over 400 of them would be directly involved in the project. The remainder would result from spinoffs from the economic activity. The Special Parliamentary Committee on SDI concluded: "The Committee has not received evidence that government participation would result in significant job creation in Canada in the research phase of the SDI.''

Furthermore, the fact that military spending doesn't greatly assist civilian technological development applies here as much as with the Cruise. As a recent study by the New York-based Council on Economic Priorities noted, the commercial utility of such SDI-associated technologies as particle beams, laser optics, infra-red sensors, and high-energy lasers is "not immediately obvious." Senior officials of the huge IBM and Siemens corporations — both heavily involved in high-tech research — told a European audience (June 1985) that there will be no relevant civilian industrial spinoffs from SDI. This will be particularly true for Canada, given that Canadian involvement in U.S. military programs has almost always been at the low end of the military technology scale — Canada gets the "scraps." It must also be remembered (as discussed in Chapter 5) that Canada-U.S. military industrial reciprocity has been institutionalized in the Defense Production Sharing Arrangement. In the long term, Canadian military exports to the U.S. (including research contracts such as the ones that would come via Star Wars) must be matched by military imports from the United States. While the balance may temporarily shift, over the long term there will be no net benefit.

From the Pentagon's point of view, it hardly matters whether Canadian know-how is employed in SDI research, so long as Canadian political support holds. But while the research phase does not rely on Canadian participation, an actual space defense system certainly would.

The North Warning System

The DEW-Line, a string of radar stations across the Canadian north, was allowed to become obsolete during the mid-1970s. As the major threat became intercontinental ballistic missiles, the U.S. no longer saw a need for an active defense system against bombers. A 1975 Congressional Research Service report concluded: "Even a 100 per cent effective defense against bombers, in the absence of anti-ballistic missile defenses, would be of little value."

In an oddly prophetic brief presented to the Canadian government in 1977, Colin Gray (now a major proponent of SDI) noted that there was then no doctrinal demand for an upgraded system:

> The only strategic context wherein a far more effective anti-bomber defense would be justifiable, would be one wherein you planned to win/survive World War III. This presumes a first strike by the *United States*. In the event that the U.S. struck first, eliminating 95 to 97 per cent of Soviet ICBMs and a somewhat lesser percentage of Soviet ballistic missile firing submarines, and most Soviet bombers — then an undamaged NORAD could indeed reduce considerably the amount of damage to be wrought upon North America. For reasons too obvious to mention, this scenario is not favoured in NORAD defense statements.

By the 1980s however, reasons for upgrading the early warning system were being discussed. During the 1984 air-defense hearings of the Canadian Senate's Special Committee on National Defense, a number of governmental and non-governmental witnesses stressed that a weak surveillance and early warning system could theoretically provide an adversary with a no-warning "precursor raid" option. As the Senate Report on Canada's Territorial Air Defense subsequently noted, such a strike against vital command, control and communications facilities could leave American strategic forces "decapitated, confused, unable to obtain orders and incapable of retaliating." Receiving the most publicity was the Senate's finding that the existing air defense system was "outdated and obsolete," allowing the Soviet bombers to fly "almost undetected into the heart of North America to launch a surprise attack." The existence of an effective early warning system would indicate to the Soviet Union that it would have nothing to gain from attempting an air-borne pre-emptive strike, since the early warning would activate American retaliatory forces.

Canada agreed in 1985 to pay forty per cent of the $1.2-billion cost of upgrading the antiquated Distant Early Warning Line into the new North Warning System. The rest of the cost will be borne by Washington. What some critics fear is that NWS will indeed be a warning system — one that warns against Soviet missiles launched in retaliation against an American first strike. How deeply will the Canadian north and the North Warning System be drawn into U.S. strategic defense plans?

The fear that NWS will become part of a new American anti-ballistic missile system is, for the immediate future, unfounded. NWS is a passive system designed to give early warning of an "air-breathing" (piloted aircraft and unpiloted Cruise missiles) attack from the Soviet Union. It will not have the capacity to detect incoming ballistic missiles, nor will it have the ability to attack incoming aircraft. On these terms NWS will identify intrusions into Canadian air space and make undetected pre-emptive strikes against U.S. retaliatory forces impossible, thus enhancing deterrence. Ground-based radars in the Canadian north have no utility in the development of either a space-based or ground-based ballistic missile defense system.

NWS only begins to resemble a Trojan horse if the implications of a successful SDI scheme are considered. If the ballistic missile threat were neutralized by the SDI satellite-based defense system, the Soviets would likely shift their emphasis to Cruise missiles, which SDI could not defend against. These would be targeted to go through ''the back door'' in Canada's north. North American air defenses would increase in importance. The U.S. might move to incorporate the Canadian north into a general strategic defense posture in order to seal defenses before the Soviets make their move.

Evidence that this scenario is being taken into account in Washington is available from both the statements of influential analysts and leaders, and from the funding of some fledgling research projects. The general inspiration for a broader strategic defense plan was outlined by Keith Payne and Colin Gray in *Foreign Affairs*:

> In essence, what would be involved would be a new direction in U.S. nuclear policy, involving a serious commitment to strategic defensive forces. Of course, such a commitment could not limit itself to countering the threat from ballistic missiles, but would also call for greatly improved capabilities to defend against strategic bomber and Cruise missile threats.

In this vein, a senior U.S. Air Force official has said of SDI: "If you're going to fix the roof, you don't want to leave the doors and windows wide open."

U.S. arms control advisor Paul Nitze, while on a visit to Ottawa in March of 1985, refused to rule out the possibility that NWS could become a part of SDI. During an appearance on Canadian television, U.S. Defense Secretary Weinberger said that missile launchers could be placed in Canada to shoot down Soviet bombers or air-launched Cruise missiles. "Some might be here [in Canada]," said Weinberger. "It just depends on where is the most effective technical place for them to be put." Finally, Robert S. Cooper, head of the U.S. Defense Advanced Research Projects Agency, has remarked: "It makes no sense to provide a robust system to intercept ICBMs and ignore the threat of long-range Cruise missiles." He went on to say that "the problem of long-range acquisition of Cruise missile aircraft and bringing those aircraft under attack before they can disgorge their load of Cruise missiles is particularly important — and space systems are the only way of accomplishing that purpose."

There are two research projects underway directed at closing the "doors and windows" to the Soviet Cruise. SDI director Lt. Gen. James Abrahamson told Congress early in 1984 that he is looking at means of developing effective Cruise missile defense. Two Canadian firms — Spar Aerospace Ltd. of Toronto and Canadian Astronautics of Ottawa — have received Canadian defense contracts of $900,000 each to study the feasibility of space-based radar surveillance systems to detect Cruise missiles and bombers. The connections to President Reagan's Strategic Defense Initiative have been denied, but the connection to strategic defense in general is inescapable.

As well, the U.S. Army has hired four American defense contractors to design a new weapon that technically would have to be land-based in the far north.

The secret project, codenamed "Braduskill," calls for the creation of a defensive missile that would intercept Soviet missiles in outer space, fly alongside, and fire explosive warheads at them. Experts in Washington speculate that the new missile would be a form of unmanned interceptor rocket, capable of firing a variety of guided missiles, energy beams or explosive projectiles. Its weapons would be guided to their targets by infra-red sensing devices or radar-sensitive homing instruments. But to be effective, the experts say, hundreds of the missiles would have to be based close to the Soviet Union, most likely in the Canadian north. "If I was the manager of this contract, I would be extremely disappointed if the contractors on this project don't look at Canada as the most likely base for these weapons," remarked John Pike, associate director of space policy for the Federation of American Scientists, which is opposed to U.S. Star Wars plans. By Pentagon spending standards, the $1 million allotted in brainstorming contracts for Braduskill is small potatoes. *Defense Week*, a Washington-based military affairs newsletter, reports that U.S. Army officials are "enthusiastic" about the project's potential. "Only by being located in Canada, along the line of flight of Soviet missiles, could a ground-based interceptor catch up with the missile in time to shoot it down before it re-entered the atmosphere," says the newsletter, quoting non-government U.S. sources.

Cruise-missile test flights over Canada are also expected to be used to test a new U.S. Air Force spy satellite that will play a role in Star Wars. During January of 1986, when the U.S. Air Force launches its first top-secret military space shuttle flight from Vandenburg Air Force Base in California, American scientists will send a super-sophisticated spy satellite,

"Teal Ruby," into orbit over Canada's far north. The satellite, developed over ten years at a cost of $241 million, carries infra-red sensors designed to detect Soviet strategic bombers and low-flying Cruise missiles as they fly across the Canadian north. While Teal Ruby is not officially part of the Star Wars program, Pentagon documents say the new satellite will provide the groundwork for a whole series of Star Wars research projects. Its research will be used in developing the space-based laser and Air Force programs as well as in developing an Air Force advanced warning system, an Air Force-based surveillance system, and a Navy integrated tactical surveillance system.

It is noteworthy that the way has already been cleared to some extent for Canadian participation in missile defense. When the NORAD pact renewal was drawn up, it contained a paragraph explicitly excluding Canadian involvement in missile defense, which was inserted on Canada's request. This limited Canadian involvement to bomber defense. However, in 1981 this paragraph was removed from the pact, the reason being that the Anti-Ballistic Missile Treaty between the superpowers had made the paragraph obsolete. This does not quite ring true, since the ABM Treaty was signed in 1972 and the paragraph was left in during the reviews of the NORAD pact in 1973 and 1975. Skeptical observers, including Allan McKinnon, Tory defense minister in 1979-80, believe that government officials knew in 1981 that space-based defensive systems were on the horizon and wanted to keep their policy options open, possibly with respect to an upgraded DEW-Line. McKinnon stated: "I think the defense establishment wanted [MPs] to have no reservations about getting involved in outer space technology." If inclusion of a provision in the 1967 NORAD pact signalled Canada's clear intention not to participate in NORAD's ballistic missile defense role, then the dropping of the provision in 1981 at a time of resurgent interest in ballistic missile defense signalled that the question was open again.

If the United States deployed a ballistic missile defense system, not only would Canada likely be involved through NORAD at a command and control level, but the U.S. might, as Weinberger revealed, request permission to deploy parts of the system in Canada. Robin Ranger noted in his study of the implications for NORAD of U.S. deployment of an ABM system:

> Given the importance to the North American defense of obtaining the earliest, and most accurate, information possible on the precise size and trajectory of a Soviet ICBM strike ... the U.S. would seem likely to have considerable interest in utilizing Canadian territory for sensors such as the overlay systems Forward Acquisition Sensor System.

Can Canada continue to participate in NORAD's early warning system without becoming involved in ballistic missile defense? In a ballistic missile defense system, early warning devices would become targeting devices. They would be particularly important in systems intended to destroy attacking missiles in their initial boost phase. In his 1984 testimony to a Senate committee, Dr. George Lindsay, chief of the Department of National Defense's Operational Research and Analysis Establishment, stated:

> The defense against air attack, including Cruise missiles, will be the responsibility of NORAD. Canada will be involved in the planning and execution and

> Canadian air space will be a primary area.... Should ballistic missile defense be deployed, it would be operationally desirable to place it under the operational control of NORAD. In general, it seems likely that a boost-phase intercept system would be based in space and a terminal-phase intercept system in the United States. For mid-course interception, it is possible that it would be desirable, perhaps even essential, to locate certain sensors, readout stations or launchers in Canada.

The North Warning System accord could lead to Canada's eventual overt participation in U.S. offensive military strategy. Crisis provisions in the accord allow eight Airborne Warning and Control System (AWACS) planes on Canadian territory in an emergency. As well, the agreement paves the way for the upgrading of a dozen landing strips across the Canadian Arctic for the forward deployment of U.S. F-15 fighter-interceptors in the event of a NORAD alert. According to U.S. nuclear critic William Arkin, "Canadians clearly don't have access to our war plans. The Canadian government clearly doesn't know what we have up our sleeve. It's another aspect of the way Canada is a nuclear colony of the United States."

The obvious danger is that Canada will be called upon to go well beyond early warning to provide Canadian territory and facilities to develop the capacity to shoot down Soviet bombers and Cruise missiles. It is noteworthy that the projected modernization does not yet provide for the essentials of a modern active air defense. That would involve far more interceptor aircraft (with full anti-Cruise capabilities), far more early-warning sensors (land- and space-based), far more AWACS-type aircraft, dramatically improved command and control facilities, surface-to-air missile batteries and, to counter the threat from submarine-launched Cruise missiles, dramatically improved anti-submarine warfare capabilities. What is of immediate concern is that northern surveillance may open the door to large numbers of interceptor aircraft.

Such a development would undermine deterrence. Comprehensive northern air defense operations in Canada would not be there to protect American second-strike weapons from a pre-emptive Soviet strike. Rather, like the deployment of first-strike capable systems such as the MX or Trident D-5 missiles, comprehensive northern air defense would be designed to limit Soviet retaliatory capacity. In other words, American strategic defense, whether space-based or air-borne, is intended to enhance American war-fighting options, not to bolster deterrence. Soviet strategic defense initiatives are, of course, destabilizing in the same way.

Since the world cannot afford the risk of undermining deterrence, the upgrading of northern surveillance in Canada must be de-coupled from SDI. On this front alone, Canada has a leading role to play in the question of Star Wars. It is Canadian sovereign territory and air space that is required for either Canadian or American interceptor aircraft in the north. What happens or does not happen in the Canadian north will have a direct effect on U.S. strategic defense, and by extension on U.S. first-strike objectives.

When "No" Means "Yes"

On September 9, 1985, Canada formally declined the U.S. offer to participate in SDI on a government-to-government basis. However, Prime Minister Mulroney's qualified "no" to Star Wars is in fact a "yes."

His statement not only endorsed the U.S. SDI program, but also paved the way for direct Canadian industrial involvement — with government assistance. Just as with the Cruise — and military production in general — Canadian firms are being encouraged to bid on SDI research through the facilities of the Defense Production Sharing Arrangement. Canadian research activities can be subsidized with public money through the Defense Industry Productivity Programme.

The Conservative government made it very clear from the outset of the Star Wars review (by a committee of MPs and Senators) that it had no intention of regulating the private sector's "freedom" to bid on Star Wars contracts. Defense Minister Erik Nielsen argued that a ban on such research contracts "would be a terrible impediment to place in the way of the free enterprise system in this country and on Canadian companies." From another point of view, this means individual private companies are sovereign on a major national question. Nine of the top ten American companies receiving Pentagon SDI research contracts have subsidiaries in Canada and, according to New Democrat MP Stephen Langdon, the Canadian affiliates could easily get involved in SDI without trying. Other corporations, of course, may also try to acquire SDI work. The infrastructure for corporate involvement — with government subsidy — is already in place. In addition to DIPP grants, the Canadian Commercial Corporation (a federal crown corporation) will mediate SDI contracts for Canadian firms, and the Defense Programs Branch of External Affairs will likely search out Star Wars work for Canada. Defense Minister Nielsen has acknowledged that the government would not prohibit the National Research Council from entering joint ventures with private firms on SDI contracts. All of this amounts to direct Canadian government involvement with Star Wars — a "yes" through the back door.

The Canadian arms industry claims that the government's formal "no" to the American offer will severely jeopardize its ability to get SDI contracts. Supposedly, classified research work will be denied to Canadian firms. Canadian business may now get a smaller slice of the SDI pie, but the underlying reality is that Canada would have received very little in the way of Star Wars research contracts in any case, because of heavy pressure in the U.S. to keep the contracts at home and the limited technological sophistication of Canadian industry.

The Canadian decision of an apparent "no" was made to placate strong disarmament feelings throughout the country without offending Washington. The government couldn't afford to take an unequivocal "yes" position as the disarmament movement has become a force to be reckoned with. However, Ottawa's loyalty remains with the Reagan administration. Liberal MP Warren Allmand complained that "The Prime Minister's decision reminds me of Pontius Pilate, who washed his hands and said he would not condemn Christ to death but left the mob free to do so."

The Risks of SDI

Canadian public opinion is divided on Star Wars. Many would support the view of the Aerospace Industries Association of Canada, which maintains that "Canada's acceptance of the U.S. invitation to participate in the research phase of the Strategic Defense Initiative is so logically correct that opposition to it, we believe, can stand only on emotional grounds." On the other hand, many would agree with the Canadian Centre for Arms Control and Disarmament, which argues:

> While SDI is unlikely to "render nuclear weapons impotent and obsolete," in President Reagan's words, strategic defenses could well act to render assured retaliation impotent and obsolete. This is no small adjustment to the world of deterrence as we have come to know it. It threatens to eliminate the bedrock of stable deterrence — the sobering knowledge on both sides that retaliation would be swift, sure, and utterly destructive....

What the latter view recognizes is that there is no quick fix that will end the arms race, no technological gimmick that will neutralize our nuclear problem. Talk of a space-based anti-missile shield over the United States only risks speeding up and destabilizing the arms race. Though there is little satisfaction to be taken in the current international situation, where the guarantee of survival rests precariously on a guarantee of mutual destruction, those elements that have provided relative peace should be preserved. One such element is the doctrine of mutual deterrence as embodied in the terms of the 1972 ABM Treaty.

The claim that the U.S. must proceed with a massive research program because the USSR has been conducting research and testing is part of the mind-set that has prevailed for four decades and brought the superpowers to this critical moment in history. If both nations are guilty, but neither has yet achieved a dangerous advantage over the other, is this not the time to move for a ban on all testing of space weapons, thus preventing destabilizing developments by either side?

Failing such an initiative, Star Wars will work at cross-purposes with arms control and disarmament.

218 Misguided Missiles

Professor Hans Bethe, who worked on the Manhattan Project during World War II and won a Nobel Prize in physics in 1967, has stated:

> If it is really our objective to reduce the exposure of our population to nuclear weapons, we must avoid a commitment to global BMD, for that will produce precisely the opposite result: a large expansion of nuclear forces aimed against us, combined with a vastly complex defensive system whose performance will remain a deep mystery until the tragic moment when it will be called into action.

To believe that an adequate shield against nuclear attack is possible requires an extravagant faith in concepts of high-technology defense, together with an extravagantly pessimistic assessment of the offensive developments which would undoubtedly accompany any BMD initiative. To believe that SDI would help to stabilize the arms race is to believe that the Kremlin would allow the U.S. to make itself invulnerable to attack while at the same time perfecting offensive systems which could pulverize Soviet targets with impunity. In fact, the Russians would not only vastly increase the number and variety of their missiles and warheads, but would also improve their quality, develop new ways of delivering them, and deploy counter-weapons, such as anti-satellite systems, to thwart American defenses. It is difficult to imagine a more hazardous confrontation. Robert Bowman, former head of the U.S. Air Force's Advanced Weapons Program, has summarized the critique of SDI proposals:

> All have staggering technical problems. All are likely to cost in the order of a trillion dollars. All violate one or more existing treaties. All are extremely vulner-

able. All are subject to a variety of countermeasures. All could be made impotent by alternative offensive missiles and therefore would be likely to reignite the numerical arms race in offensive weapons. All would, if they worked, be more effective as part of a first strike than against one. Most importantly, all would be extremely destabilizing, probably triggering the nuclear war which both sides are trying to prevent.

Canada, along with other Western nations, has been in the midst of determining its response to Star Wars. Sound advice was given by the *Globe and Mail* in an editorial of February 22, 1985:

> The Western leaders who boast of their friendship with the U.S. do it no favour when they remain silent about the peril of SDI's progress. They merely acquiesce in ill-advised efforts which undermine the fragile framework of arms control — and which abandon the proven formula of nuclear deterrence in favor of the chimera of invulnerability.
>
> Worst of all, by seeking to share in the industrial benefits of the SDI enterprise, the Western leaders who are silent about SDI's risks today ensure that their countries will be too intertwined with its development to protest when the consequences eventually become alarming and apparent.

In the final analysis, the real question is not whether Canada will participate in Star Wars. It is what Canada can do to persuade the United States to discontinue its SDI program. Opposition to SDI is still strong in the U.S. — both in the society at large and in the Congress.

After all, Star Wars is by no means a fait accompli. Reagan's $26 billion SDI program is but a drop in the bucket considering that a full-fledged Star Wars "defense" could cost up to $1 trillion. If pushed by strong public opinion, the U.S. Congress could reduce SDI allotments. The opposition of Western nations to Star Wars could have a marked effect on both public opinion and politicians in the U.S. It is not inconceivable that Star Wars could be rolled back in the 1988 presidential elections.

Conclusion: Toward a Canadian Initiative

Until recently, scientific studies indicated that nuclear war would not necessarily lead to the end of the world. Now, ironically, nuclear war has become more thinkable at the very time that it has emerged that these studies overlooked the greatest danger of all: "nuclear winter."

The nuclear winter thesis holds that an exchange of just 500 to 2,000 strategic nuclear weapons would, aside from killing a majority of the citizens of the warring states, kick so much dust, smoke and poisonous gas into the atmosphere that the planet would be turned into a dark, icy wasteland incapable of sustaining any survivors. If it was ever in doubt before, it is now abundantly clear that the global build-up of nuclear armaments has reached the point where weapons and strategies endanger what they are intended to save.

Yet President Reagan, through his "rearm America" program, is dramatically increasing nuclear-weapons spending in order, as he put it, to "lower the level of armaments" at some later date. This seems unlikely, as does the prospect of a breakthrough in arms control negotiations so long as Washington insists that it will not abandon its Strategic Defense Initiative in exchange for cuts, however large, in the Soviet nuclear arsenal. The American posture essentially is carrying out the recommendation of Reagan advisor Edwin Meese that arms control should be subject to "benign neglect" while the U.S. goes about the business of re-arming. This is hardly surprising, since Reagan campaigned on "Peace Through Strength," remarking that "I've never seen anyone insult Jack Dempsey."

That may be so, but the person who might have disliked Dempsey did not have thousands of nuclear warheads at home. And the history of the arms race reveals that the Soviets will strive to keep pace with the Americans.

Both countries are now beginning to deploy a new generation of more accurate and deadly nuclear weapons which will reduce warning time, make the other side's land-based nuclear forces more vulnerable, and increase both the pressure for launch-on-warning strategies and the likelihood of a war sparked by accident or anticipation. The doctrine of nuclear war-fighting and the "continuum of options" has only raised the risk. Even more destabilizing developments, such as the militarization of space, loom on the horizon. These pressures are making the world a much more dangerous place than it has been at any time since the dawn of the nuclear age. Some decision-makers are convinced war is inevitable: former Reagan advisor Eugene Rostow declares "We live in pre-war not post-war times!"

The prospects for arms control and disarmament are bleak. But strategies for disarmament are not lacking.

What is lacking is political will. As in a Greek tragedy, the nations of the world can see nuclear war coming, but they can't muster the resolve to stop it. There has been a failure to acknowledge the simple fact that at this point in the arms race, increases in weaponry do not enhance the security of anyone, but reduce the security of everyone. George Kennan has captured the essence of this quandary:

> I believe that until we consent to recognize that the nuclear weapons we hold in our own hands are as much a danger to us as those that repose in the hands of our supposed adversaries there will be no escape from the confusions and dilemmas to which such weapons have now brought us, and must bring us increasingly as time goes on.

Only a very radical reduction of existing arms stockpiles could, in a purely physical sense, make the world safer. It has been estimated that either superpower could start dismantling its nuclear weapons at an ante of ten per cent per year, and still be able to destroy the other superpower several times over after twenty years. While the ultimate goal of complete nuclear disarmament is obviously very far way, the commencement of the first stages is imperative if the immediate danger posed by the movement into first-strike weapons and doctrine is to be contained.

The Price of Arms

One of the many ironies of the arms build-up was illuminated by E. P. Thompson's remark about Star Wars: "At astronomic cost, an astral venture will be set in motion to achieve an end — the blocking of each other's missiles — which could be achieved tomorrow, at no cost at all, by a rational agreement by both parties to disarm."

The ultimate cost of an American Star Wars scheme will be between $500 billion and $1,000 billion (or $1 trillion). This money will be spent at a time when two billion people suffer from malnutrition and at least 150 million of them are starving. Every minute in 1985, thirty children throughout the world died from lack of food and health care. And every minute, $1 million was consumed by military budgets. The world's total military bill in 1985 was $1 trillion; $200 billion of it went toward nuclear arms.

Military spending by northern countries obviously contributes to global insecurity. But the diversion of resources from human needs to the instruments of war is in itself a cause of conflict. Many equations have been formulated to illustrate this. For instance, Pierre Trudeau told the United Nations in 1978 that "If we decided to use for peaceful purposes the amount we spend in two weeks for military purposes, we could provide drinking water and basic health care to the population of the entire world." Famine and impoverishment in the Third World will likely be the cause of increasing world tension, and will serve as the trigger for superpower military conflict. The failure to arrest malnutrition, disease, illiteracy — indeed the whole range of conditions that describes underdevelopment — is the legacy of an arms race that not only misuses scarce resources but also sustains and entrenches an unjust international economic order. The common welfare of nations urgently requires an initiative for economic and political security on the scale of the Strategic Defense Initiative. As the Talmud (a collection of post-biblical Jewish thought) warns: "the sword comes into the world from justice too long delayed."

The 1967 Outer Space Treaty proclaimed "the common interest of all mankind ... in the use of outer space for peaceful purposes." Instead of being subverted for military uses, space technology could solve many of the world's pressing problems. Remote-sensing devices can pinpoint subterranean water in arid regions, identify locust swarms and crop diseases, and speed geological exploration. Direct broadcasting satellites have opened up new vistas in rural education. Communication satellites can boost trade and provide navigational assistance to merchant fleets and aircraft. Meteorological satellites improve food production and transport safety by helping to predict the weather.

How could this conversion be begun? A direct and safe road is there for all to see: equitable and verifiable deep cuts in strategic offensive forces to below the number that would trigger a nuclear winter, immediate negotiations to ban all space weapons, and the introduction of conventional alternatives to nuclear weapons.

Canada's Role

It is true that Canada is a minor player in the nuclear arms race in terms of actual participation. But for the superpowers the political support of allies is often more critical than the sort of specific auxiliary services that Canada provides. This was illustrated by the furor that greeted the refusal by New Zealand — a country a fraction the size of Canada, and much less important in U.S. military plans — to allow nuclear-armed U.S. submarines in its ports.

Geographic, economic and political circumstances place Canada in a unique position of influence and responsibility as the U.S. presses ahead with plans for first strikes, nuclear war-fighting, and space-based defense. Coming from its closest neighbour and respected ally, Canadian initiatives could profoundly affect the U.S. They would also make an impression on other Western allies who collectively could bring enormous pressure to bear on Washington.

And a Canadian intervention would come at a time when there is a desperate need for a *new* voice for peace. The U.S. and USSR both stress the ugliest features of the other's society and both are locked into preconceptions that impede the pursuit of their mutual interest in disarmament. Canada can fill the critical role of "third negotiator" identified by E. P. Thompson. The need for such a catalyst has been widely recognized. Robert Oppenheimer, one of those responsible for the development of the nuclear bomb, compared the superpowers to two scorpions in a bottle who will kill each other — unless the bottle is smashed from the outside.

Would unilateral Canadian measures do more harm than good by dividing the Western alliance? As we've seen at various points in this book, the NATO alliance is not a monolith. And it should not be, unless the member nations wish to have as little independence as their counterparts in the Warsaw Pact. After all, there is no question of whether Canada is an ally of the U.S.; nor is there any doubt that the USSR, with its 8,000-plus strategic nuclear weapons, poses a threat to international stability. The choice is not between the U.S. and the USSR but between disarmament and extinction. If Canada is to become part of the solution rather than part of the problem, it cannot go on participating in systems such as the Cruise, for in so doing Canada joins the U.S. in sending messages to Moscow that the Americans are intent on achieving a war-fighting capability.

Peace initiatives are often dismissed on the basis that unilateral measures amount to appeasement. This argument avoids the nature of the unilateral initiatives now being proposed. As a leader of the Netherlands Interchurch Peace Council put it, a unilateral step "should be drastic enough to be a clear expression of an alternative approach, but at the same time small enough to enable allies and others to respond to it on the military and political level." Canada, as a strategically minor but politically important partner in the Western alliance, is in an ideal position to make such moves. A Canadian initiative could include ending Cruise testing in Canada; withdrawing from the Defense Development and Production Sharing Arrangement; supporting the call for a nuclear freeze; working for a NATO "no-first-use" declaration; opposing SDI and prohibiting participation by Canadian firms; and refusing to allow the North Warning System to be drawn into first-use planning. These measures would have a profound impact on the intellectual lockjaw of the superpowers without undermining the Western deterrent, which after all, is of overwhelming dimensions.

Clearly, a Canadian peace initiative would demand a more independent Canadian foreign policy — which means greater independence from the policies of the U.S. This seems unlikely to happen as long as the Mulroney government remains proudly pro-American, and seeks to end the "certain strains of confrontation" created under the Liberals. So as not to disturb the "special relationship" with the U.S., Minister of External Affairs Joe Clark declined in 1984 to ask the USSR and the U.S. to consider banning Cruise missiles from their arsenals. The Conservatives have been so careful to give Washington the "benefit of the doubt" that even Pierre Trudeau — whose own government's orientation toward American foreign policy was described by Minister of External Affairs Mark MacGuigan as "quiet acquiescence" — challenged Brian Mulroney to "stop kowtowing" to the U.S.

Clearly too, the initiative must rely on actual Canadian measures like the ones described. Pierre Trudeau flatly stated, "The people of Canada want peace. They don't care what the Pentagon says," and mounted his famous peace initiative. But as Albert Einstein once remarked, "Mere praise of peace is easy, but ineffective." Trudeau carried out his campaign as if there was no incongruity in lecturing the superpowers while Canada carried on with Cruise testing and component production. This kind of contradiction is gaining Canada a reputation for "talking big and doing nothing" about the arms race, in the words of Norwegian peace researcher John Galtung.

The charges that meet suggestions to disentangle Canada from American rearmament — of breaking alliance solidarity, of appeasement and anti-Americanism — have been used throughout the nuclear age, and will always have a strong emotional appeal, even if they have no obvious basis in fact. But increasing numbers of people from all nations and in all walks of life are now recognizing the circular logic of the arms race, and would welcome a Canadian resolve to go against the tide. Even within the top military, scientific and political circles directly involved in the arms race (if not among munitions makers), there is now a strong voice of dissent. Perhaps no better example can be given than this 1984 statement on Star Wars by the thirteen members (including retired Canadian Major General Leonard Johnson) of Generals for Peace:

> Let there be no illusion about space weapons: they are not for "Star Wars" but for nuclear war on Earth. Space weapons combined with offensive nuclear missiles, such as MX, Pershing II and Trident II, destroy the opponent's second-strike capability, thus making possible a first strike. A first strike capability leads with certainty to war. We resolutely demand: let us not continue the insanity of the arms race by extending into space. Let us instead unite our creative energies in the struggle against hunger and poverty for the reconciliation of humanity!

The abandonment of Canada's participation in the development of nuclear weapons would be a chink in the arms race, a sign that the endless escalation of nuclear weaponry can be checked. It is not too late to stop SDI; and the weapons that support the doctrine of war-fighting and first use are only in the early stages of deployment. As scientist and disarmament specialist John C. Polanyi has said: "There is a limit to what one country can do to stem the tide of weapons development. However, history is giving Canada a brief moment on the stage. If we fail to use it wisely, history will not view us kindly. Nor should it."

Glossary: Nuclear Weapons Terminology and Policy Bodies

ABM: Anti-ballistic missile, a system for destroying ballistic missiles.

ABM Treaty: A Salt-I document which puts restrictions on ABM interceptors, launchers, and radar.

ACM: Advanced Cruise missile, a new generation of Cruise now being developed, perhaps employing "stealth" technology to evade radar.

ALCM: Air-launched Cruise missile, one of three types of Cruise missile. The ALCM is launched from a bomber, and has an intercontinental range.

Arms Control and Disarmament Agency: An agency of the U.S. Department of State.

Arms Control Association: non-partisan Washington-based organization dedicated to promoting public understanding of effective policies and programs in arms control and disarmament.

ASAT: Anti-satellite weapon.

AWACS: Airborne Warning and Control System. An air-based defense system carrying radar, navigation and communication equipment designed to detect, track and intercept attacking aircraft.

BMD: Ballistic missile defense, a system designed to destroy offensive strategic ballistic missiles or their warheads in flight.

Brookings Institution: A non-partisan Washington-based think tank.

Bulletin of Atomic Scientists: A monthly American magazine of science and world affairs.

Canadian Centre for Arms Control and Disarmament: Ottawa-based institute established to provide independent, non-partisan research.

CANUSTEP: Canada-United States Test and Evaluation Program, under which the Cruise missile is tested.

Centre for Defense Information: Research body founded by dissident group of senior military officers opposed to Pentagon arms buildup.

Deterrence: A nuclear strategy whereby a potential aggressor is "deterred" from attacking because of the massive and unacceptable retaliation that would follow.

DEW-Line: Distant Early Warning Line. NORAD system of radars intended to detect incoming warheads and bombers. Currently being modernized into the North Warning System.

DIPP: Defense Industry Productivity Programme. A program of the federal government which gives corporations grants to help them convert to military production.

DND: Department of National Defense (Canada).

DPSA: Defense Production Sharing Arrangement. Through the DPSA, Canadian defense contractors gain access to sub-contracts for components of American weapons projects. The name was recently changed to Defense Development and Production Sharing Arrangement.

First-strike Capability: The ability to conduct a disarming first strike against one's opponent.

GLCM: Ground-launched Cruise missile. Medium range, fired from launchers. The Cruise missiles deployed in Europe are GLCMs.

Hudson Institute: A "right wing" American think tank which has been influential in advancing U.S. rearmament programs.

ICBM: Intercontinental ballistic missile. A missile with a range in excess of 3,400 miles. The MX, now being developed, is an American example.

Independent Commission on Disarmament and Security Issues: A group of international government officials which convened in 1980 and reported in 1982.

INF: Intermediate-Range Nuclear Forces, subdivided into long-range — over 600 miles (for instance, so-called Eurostrategic weapons); medium-range; and short-range — up to 120 miles (also referred to as tactical or battlefield nuclear weapons).

Laser: A device that emits a beam of light composed of nearly parallel rays. Three types of lasers are under consideration by the U.S. Department of Defense as anti-ICBM weapons: chemical lasers which emit infra-red light, excimer lasers which emit ultraviolet light, and lasers pumped by X-rays emitted by a nuclear explosion.

MAD: Mutually assured destruction. In theory, the deterrent against a nuclear first-strike.

MIRV: Multiple Independent Targetable Re-entry Vehicle. Two or more re-entry vehicles carried by a ballistic missile, each of which can be individually directed toward a separate target.

MX: Missile Experimental (dubbed the "Peacekeeper" by President Reagan). When deployed in the late 1980s will be the most accurate ICBM.

NASA: National Aeronautics and Space Administration.

NATO: North Atlantic Treaty Organization, the military alliance of North American and West European states.

NORAD: North American Aerospace Defense Command. A combined U.S.-Canadian command responsible for the detection of any missile or bomber attack on North America. Notably, the name has been revised from the original to replace "air" with "aerospace."

NWS: North Warning System, upgrade of the outdated DEW-Line.

Operation Dismantle: Ottawa-based peace lobby, whose main objective is a global referendum on disarmament.

Particle beams: Intense beams of subatomic particles, usually electrons, capable of destroying animate objects.

Pershing II: An extremely accurate intermediate-range nuclear weapon being deployed by the United States in Western Europe.

Poseidon: A class of U.S. ballistic missile-launching submarines.

Project Ploughshares: Canadian disarmament and development lobby and research group. A project of Canadian churches and development agencies.

Re-entry Vehicles (RVs): That part of a ballistic missile designed to carry a nuclear warhead and to re-enter the earth's atmosphere after the missile has completed its trajectory in space.

Stockholm International Peace Research Institute: An independent military research institute.

SALT: Strategic Arms Limitation Talks. SALT I began in 1969 and ended in 1972 with the ABM Treaty.

SALT II was never ratified by the U.S., but both sides claim to live up to its provisions.

SDI: Strategic Defense Initiative, the official name for President Reagan's "Star Wars" research program.

SLCM: Sea-launched Cruise missile. There are currently three U.S. models.

SS-20: A Soviet intermediate-range ballistic missile being deployed against Western Europe.

Strategic Missiles: Intercontinental missiles or ICBMs, — those which can be fired from the USSR toward American targets or vice versa.

TERCOM: Terrain Contour Matching, a terrain-following navigation system used in U.S. Cruise missiles.

TNF: Theatre Nuclear Forces; in contrast to strategic, or intercontinental, nuclear missiles, TNF involves short- and medium-range missiles to be used within a "theatre," such as Europe.

Trident: The new sea leg of the U.S. strategic triad. The new submarine is called Trident. The first and second generation missiles are called Trident-1 (C-4) and Trident-2 (D-5) respectively.

Union of Concerned Scientists: A high-profile group of scientists which has been prominent in the opposition to Star Wars.

U.S. Institute for Policy Studies: A "left-wing" American think tank which develops alternative foreign policy.

Other Books in the Canadian Issues Series

Canada's Colonies
A History of the Yukon and Northwest Territories
KENNETH COATES

The history of the North has received little attention — in part because of the slight status of "Canada's Colonies" in the national scheme of things, and in part because of powerful romantic images of explorers and gold miners that have governed the Canadian concept of this region. Kenneth Coates's book relates history as seen from the North, from the vibrant pre-contact cultures of the Inuit and Dene to the land claim, resource project and self-government controversies of the 1980s.

Police
Urban Policing in Canada
JOHN SEWELL

This informative primer by Canada's best-known urban reformer, John Sewell, fills the information vacuum that reduces most discussion of policing to "for" or "against." The book begins with an outline history of policing and a discussion of the "true" extent of crime. Sewell then turns to the day-to-day issues of policing, from the effectiveness of patrol work to the drawbacks of rigid police hierarchies.

"A handy elementary guide to the basics of policing today." — *Montreal Gazette*

The West
The History of a Region in Confederation
J.F. CONWAY

Since settlers first tried to eke out a living on the banks of the Red River, Western Canadians have felt that the West's place in the Canadian scheme of things is a subordinate one. John Conway's book is a history of Confederation from the point of view of the four western provinces. Conway shows that although the focus of western dissatisfaction may have changed in recent years, the root cause of having to "buy dear and sell cheap" remains.

"A must for anyone who wishes to know about the recent economic and political past of Western Canada."
— *Lethbridge Herald*

Ethics and Economics
Canada's Catholic Bishops on the Economic Crisis
GREGORY BAUM and DUNCAN CAMERON

The most talked-about political manifesto of recent years is "Ethical Reflections on the Economic Crisis," issued in early 1983 by Canada's Catholic bishops. The statement's impact reverberated through political, church and business circles because of its trenchant critique of the structural problems of Canadian society and the economy.

This book takes the issues raised by the bishops several steps further. "Ethical Reflections" is included, followed by two wide-ranging commentaries: one from an ethical point of view, by Gregory Baum; the other from an economic perspective, by Duncan Cameron. Several earlier statements by the bishops are also included as a guide to further reading on this subject.

"A major contribution to the understanding of the Canadian Church." — *Catholic New Times*

Oil and Gas
Ottawa, the Provinces and the Petroleum Industry
JAMES LAXER

For more than a decade, the oil industry and energy policy have been a central issue in Canadian economic and political life. *Oil and Gas* offers an overview of these turbulent years and fresh insight into the motives of the main players: Ottawa, Alberta and other producing provinces, the oil majors such as Imperial, the Canadian companies like Petro-Canada, the OPEC cartel and the U.S. government.

"Provocative reading" — *Canadian Public Policy*

Women and Work
Inequality in the Labour Market
PAUL PHILLIPS and ERIN PHILLIPS

Why are women still second-class citizens at work? To answer this question, Paul and Erin Phillips trace women's involvement in the paid labour market, and in labour unions, throughout Canadian history. They document the disadvantages that women face today and examine the explanations that have been forwarded for the persistence of these problems. Chapters are devoted to the effect of technological changes such as the microelectronic "chip" on women's work and to proposals for bringing about equality in the labour market.

"A fine salute to the strong body of materials on women's work that has sprung into being in the last decade." — *Toronto Star*

Regional Disparities
New Updated Edition
PAUL PHILLIPS

This is the first and only book to address the perennial problem of the gap between "have" and "have-not" provinces. In this new updated edition of his popular study, Paul Phillips examines developments such as the National Energy Program, the Alberta-Ottawa oil deal, the industrial slump in Central Canada, and the increased prospects for economic growth in resource-rich provinces.

"A concise, convincing overview."
— *Quill & Quire*

The New Canadian Constitution
DAVID MILNE

The New Canadian Constitution explains just what everyone wanted out of the constitution-making process, who got what, and what the final results mean for Canadians. Of special interest is the concluding chapter, which examines the nature of the new constitution in terms of interests, issues and accidents that shaped it, and its own strengths and weaknesses.

"... a straightforward and comprehensive narrative."
— *Globe and Mail*

Industry in Decline
RICHARD STARKS

Summing up proposals from labour, the NDP, the business community and the Science Council of Canada, Richard Starks, a financial journalist formerly

with the *Financial Post*, examines the growing consensus that Canada needs a new industrial strategy.

"The beauty of the book and its importance is its straightforward, uncomplicated, journalistic style, and its price." — *Canadian Materials*

Rising Prices

H. LUKIN ROBINSON

This book explains why prices are so high today and tells us what inflation is all about. The author defines mystifying terms like "cost-push" inflation and applies them to everyday situations.

"A masterpiece of popular economics. The book swiftly moves from the very elementary to the very complex ... without losing its readers along the way." — *Canadian Forum*

Out of Work

CY GONICK

Cy Gonick shows why the Canadian economy is failing to create jobs for all the people who want to work, and why government is unwilling to take the necessary steps to deal with the issue.

"Gonick is one of the few political scientists around who can put complicated arguments into readable English. He talks more sense in less space than any other contemporary commentator." — *Books in Canada*